SPEED!

Preceding pages: A "start" sequence recorded by a high-speed streak camera passing 24 inches of film per second.

Fascination with this sport often centers on the obvious—the pure speed. Indeed, Indy cars are the fastest racing machines in the world, capable of attaining 230 mph on the long straightaways of the Indianapolis Motor Speedway, and averaging lap speeds of 212 mph or better. But there are many other distinctions to consider.

The sleek, rear-engined, ground-effect designs of present-day competition are the most versatile ever to turn a wheel. They compete not only at Indy's "brickyard," but also on the high banks of super speedways, on tight, one-mile ovals, and at a variety of winding road courses and city-street circuits. No other form of auto racing offers such an assortment of challenges for its competitors or spectacles for its fans.

To understand the high degree of sophistication of an Indy car, one must look beneath the car's wind-tunnel-tested carbon fiber or fiberglass bodywork. Current rules simply state that cars may be no longer than 15 feet and no wider than 78.5 inches, with a minimum wheelbase of 96 inches and a maximum height of 32 inches; the maximum allowable setback of the 43-inch-wide rear wing is 35 inches. Minimum weight of a car with a turbocharged engine is 1,550 pounds, 75 pounds less if the engine is not turbocharged.

Within the limitations of size and a host of other restrictions governing horsepower and other equipment, Indy car designers create endless variations. And although yearly attempts are made by officials to control the aerodynamic downforce and reduce cornering speeds (for safety's sake), records are constantly being trimmed by the designers' innovative solutions.

The cars keep getting quicker because they are more refined. Elements such as bellhousings and gearbox trains, wishbones, rockers, damper units, and the all-important air tunnels under the car are perfected, tuned, and repositioned to exploit the allowable to the absolute maximum. This, after all, is a sport measured in millimeters as well as in miles.

SPEED!

INDY CAR RACING

Photographs by Chet Jezierski
Introduction by Paul Newman

HARRY N. ABRAMS, INC., PUBLISHERS, NEW YORK

ACKNOWLEDGMENTS

This book, a labor of love spanning eleven years, has one simple objective—to show Indy car racing the way the competitors experience it. To accomplish this, many complex problems had to be solved. In order to record the action from unique vantage points, difficult remote camera set-ups were designed to capture preconceived pictures, survive hostile environments, and bring film back intact. Drivers, crew chiefs, and officials often had to approve certain high-risk placements. Cameras intended to ride on race cars were mounted so that no possible danger could occur. Perhaps the biggest hurdle I overcame in achieving these images was acceptance. Early on I discovered that the racing fraternity is much more than just a group of competitors. It's a family. With their help, the result of my work stands as a personal statement illustrating a remarkable profession. A number of people who aided me also shared thoughts about their work and experiences; from taped conversations I have drawn the bulk of the text. I am grateful to all for their contributions:

Mr. Jack MacDonough, whose continued support and guidance throughout the project's final two seasons helped to make this book a reality.

Jon Gilchrist, my electronics wizard and friend (father of the Automated Exposure Motorized Widelux Camera), without whom so many of the book's special images would never have been taken.

Pat Maye, who believed in the project and my capabilities and was always there to lend a hand.

Michele Ritter, whose love and patience never faltered during the many years of weekends I was never home.

Also thanks to: Mario Andretti, Michael Andretti, Anheuser-Busch, Inc., Avco Motorhomes, Jack Beckley, Nigel Bennett, Ron Bell, George Bignotti, Tom Binford, Eric Broadley, Clarence Cagle, John Capels, Phil Casey, Myron Charness, Tony Cicale, Crew of the Goodyear Airship *Mayflower*, Don Cuzzocrea, Wally Dallenbach, Frankie Delroy, Keith Duckworth, Ian Dunn, Steve Edwards, Electrolux Corporation, Jack Field and family, A. J. Foyt, Richard Fried, Goodyear Airship Operations, Jerry Grobe, Carl Haas, Rouem Haffenden, Joe Hajcak, Hanna Car Wash Systems, Derek Hanna, Kirk Hanna, Don Henderson, George Heuning, Bobby Hillin, Ray Hooper, Will Hopkins, Jackie Howerton, Instrumentation Marketing Corp., Itasca Motorhomes, Adrian Jezierski, Gordon Johncock, Bill Kamphausen, Mike Kasino, Vern Kerrick, E. Leitz, Inc., Bruce Little, Shim Malone, Ray Marquette, Jack Martin, Steve McMillan, Art Meyers, Minolta Corp., Derek Mower, Multiplex Display Fixture Corp., H. Nettling, Paul Newman, Nikon Corp., Olden Camera, Tom Powel, Repco, Inc., Dave Ritter, Kirk Russell, Danielle Sacripante, Vern Schuppan, Bill Simpson, Sinar Bron, Inc., Darrell Soppe, Starcraft, Inc., Jack Starnes, Robert Sutherland, Traveland U.S.A., Al Unser, Sr., Pat Vidan, Vivitar Corp., Basil Vorolieff, Bill Vukovich, A. J. Watson, and Ron Winter.

Without the support of track officials who continually provided access, credentials, and special consideration, this book could never have been accomplished.

Most of the photographs were taken with Minolta equipment.

Designer: Raymond P. Hooper

Project Director: Robert Morton

Associate Editor: Beverly Fazio

Interviews conducted and edited by Chet Jezierski

Library of Congress Cataloging in Publication Data

Jezierski, Chet.
  Speed: Indy car racing.

  1. Indianapolis Speedway Race. I. Title.
GV1033.5.I55J49 1985   796.7′2′06877252   84-28260
ISBN 0-8109-1649-5

Printed and bound by Amilcare Pizzi, S.p.A., Milan, Italy

Front endpaper: Panoramic view of the Ontario Motor Speedway on race morning, seen from a hot-air balloon.
Back endpaper: The Goodyear airship *Mayflower* casts its shadow on Indy's "Gasoline Alley" after the crowds have gone. The picture was made with a remote camera mounted on the blimp's tail fin.

CONTRIBUTORS

HYWEL ABSALOM	ROUEM HAFFENDEN
TYLER ALEXANDER	JIM HALL
MARIO ANDRETTI	PATRICK HEAD
MICHAEL ANDRETTI	ROBIN HERD
JOHN BARNARD	GEORGE HEUNING
NIGEL BENNETT	JACKIE HOWERTON
GEORGE BIGNOTTI	GORDON JOHNCOCK
PHIL CASEY	RICK MEARS
COLIN CHAPMAN	LEO MEHL
TONY CICALE	MIKE MOSLEY
GORDON COPPUCK	DEREK MOWER
WALLY DALLENBACH	TRACEY POTTER
DENIS DAVISS	BOBBY RAHAL
SCOTT DENNISON	STEVE ROBY
KEITH DUCKWORTH	JOHNNY RUTHERFORD
STEVE EDWARDS	BILL SIMPSON
GEOFF FERRIS	TOM SNEVA
A. J. FOYT	GEORGE SNIDER
RICHARD FRIED	AL UNSER, SR.
HOWARD GILBERT	BOBBY UNSER
EUGENE GRIMM	BILL VUKOVICH
DAN GURNEY	A. J. WATSON
CARL HAAS	MICHAEL WOLTHER

CONTENTS

Designing, Building, Testing

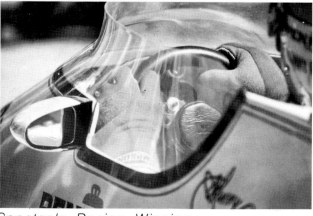

Preparations, Practice Runs, Qualifying

Spectacle, Racing, Winning

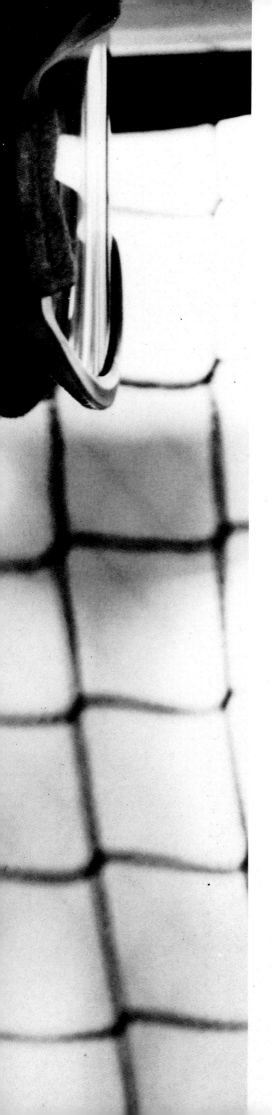

INTRODUCTION BY PAUL NEWMAN

I can't really say I had any screaming interest in driving race cars as a kid, or even in watching them. Hence, I never drove anything faster than a two-litre street Datsun until Bob Bondurant taught me to handle a CanAm for a film called *Winning*. Even then, it was four long years before I could take off a summer and get a license to race.

At first, racing was just something else to do that was fun. It wasn't all that special, and neither was I. I'm what is called a slow learner. I was a terrible actor when I started, and I was a terrible driver at first, too. The guys were calling me "old balloonfoot" behind my back. But I am persistent. So what if people giggled a little! They did it when I started acting. You learn to get laughed at and not let it drive you out of the business.

I stuck with driving, and I learned, among other things, driving isn't all that different from anything else in life. If you do it well, it makes you feel good, and you learn a few peripheral things, too—like realizing very soon that winning depends as much on what's in your head as what's under your hood. If you let yourself think another driver is better than you or quicker than you or more aggressive than you, then he's got you. It doesn't matter if his car is faster than yours or not. If you look up in the mirror and say, "Oh, Christ, here he comes," he'll beat you every time.

Intimidation is a part of racing. One can take all those ugly personality traits, like hostility and aggressiveness, out onto the track and not have to make any compromises or adjust to the other guy out there. But hostilities are left on the track. That's the part of racing that's right. It's the people, the drivers and mechanics, designers, managers, and track officials who make it all happen.

What *Speed!* has is them, the people. It has the cars, the races, and the tracks the way the drivers see them, the way the mechanics and crew chiefs see them. It catches the elegance of a pit crew in action and the way the wall looks from the cockpit, blurred by the speed. And it's told by the men who've been there, who've conceived the Indy-style racers, tested them, wrecked them, and won with them.

The championship cars in *Speed!* are a lot different from the sedans I drive. They're faster, they handle differently, and they're more dangerous. But the racing is the same and the feeling is the same. There's that special sense of union you get when you and the car are one, when you can put it through a turn getting absolutely all the adhesion that car can give you, when you can outmaneuver and outbreak and pass a tough competitor. That's what racing is all about.

Paul Newman

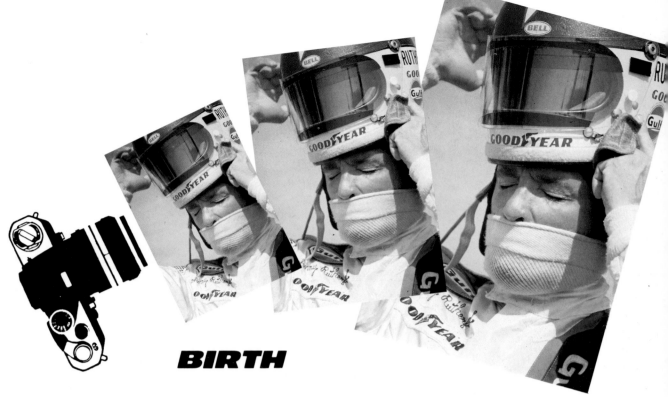

A PHOTOGRAPHER'S NOTEBOOK

BIRTH

Just as an artist often "sees" his creation upon the white surface of a fresh canvas even before he picks up a brush, so, too, the race car designer preconceives the advantages he needs to go as fast as possible within the sanctioning body's rule book. He then combines the discipline of an aerodynamicist with the sensitivity of a sculptor, first converting interpretations of his solutions into flat drawings at the drafting table.

These designs, like an architect's blueprints, take their first three-dimensional form in the model shop, where quarter-scale miniatures are carved, sanded, and assembled. Interchangeable parts—cowlings, sidepods, and undersides—can be found sitting among the wood shavings, along with modeling clay and pieces of styrofoam that may be used to make slighter modifications in the next phase of development.

During week-long sessions, usually scheduled months in advance, the designer and his assistants will test all the variables of their new configurations at a quarter-scale wind tunnel. As a stream of air is channeled over the model, twists of spaghetti-sized tubing carry surface pressure readings from numbered holes drilled into the model at key locations. Fixed in place, the miniature race car "rolls along" on its white, roller-skate-like wheels over a moving-ground plane while a computer records the data on sheets of read-outs from the probes. Different combinations of model elements, like sidepods and cowlings, enable the designer to achieve an optimum balance between maximum downforce and minimum drag, leading to a faster result on the track, where it really counts.

After a careful examination of all the numbers achieved with the model, it's time to "pencil" the car in literally hundreds of mechanical drawings that will reflect the experimental evidence gathered in the tunnel as well as the designer's years of experience. These drawings must precisely describe all the elements, every nut and bolt, of the car, so that assembly-shop personnel can fabricate them accurately.

Drawings lie draped over workbenches everywhere; the outline of major components is scribed on sheet metal for cutting; and the actual body-building process finally gets underway. A large metal table, leveled and rigged to support the growing number of pieces for the car's "tub"—that portion in which the driver sits—soon becomes the center of attention. Skillfully hammered and welded bulkheads, drilled to accommodate riveting, are fitted to large, preformed sheets of aluminum and carbon fiber that make up the shell of the vehicle; a definable shape becomes visible.

Temporary fasteners hold everything in place while each edge and measurement is rechecked. Perhaps the driver will visit the shop at this stage, crawling through the litter of tools, cardboard forms, and metal filings to climb into the tub and try it on for size. Then, a final assessment of the pedal placements and instrument-panel height gives way to the start of the gluing and riveting procedure. This can take days to finish. When completed, the tub will undergo a stress test to determine if it will resist twisting under the thousands of pounds of pressure that will be exerted upon it at, say, 205 mph.

Now the assembly-shop men turn their attention to creating the many additional elements needed to complete the car. While they work through piles of drawings, the motor that will power their creation at 290 feet per second or better is being carved out of a cast block of aluminum. In the modern Cosworth factory at Northampton, England (where some of the following pictures were made), the process is highly automated. In place on a rotating table before a computer-controlled "machining center," the raw engine block will undergo a series of precise refinements.

Afterwards, the block is moved to other work areas where it receives still more refinements by Cosworth's white-coated workers. Throughout the fortnight it takes to prepare a motor for shipment, many components are being simultaneously machined and checked for accuracy at different locations throughout the plant—cams, cranks, rods, and of course pistons, to name a few.

The in-house forging of Cosworth pistons deserves special note. Cylindrical "slugs" of metal cut from aluminum bar stock are preheated and individually placed in a huge drop forge. The hole in which the slug fits is the same shape as the outside of a piston. A punch in the shape of the inside is attached to the arm of the forge. When the operator is ready, the machine drops the punch onto the superheated slug with three to five hundred tons of pressure. This causes the pliable metal to flow like toothpaste into the desired form. As the punch is lifted, a newly formed piston sits silhouetted in the glow of its own fire and smoke, bringing to mind visions of medieval alchemy.

But the flames die out quickly, and a long set of tongs enables the operator to transfer the piston into a crate with others. When filled, the crate is pushed into the machining and grinding area, where balanced sets of eight closely matched pistons will be assembled.

The finished block, its new pistons, and many other engine parts will spend a week in the final assembly area before moving on to the last stop—the test chamber. Linked to one of Cosworth's three electronically controlled dynamometers by yards of pressure hosing and wiring, the motor for the new race car is eventually run up to full power while its vital functions are checked.

While passing its tests, the engine's fuel-injection system is set up and then the motor is crated for shipping, along with the necessary water and oil pumps. Also included are recommendations for oil tank design, plumbing arrangements, and the exhaust system.

Back at the race car shop, many hands have been occupied for many weeks welding, machining, and fabricating. By now nose sections and side pods have been attached to the tub and a dummy motor is bolted in place as a stressed member of the car. The undersides of the pods are carefully fitted and work on the turbocharger placement and exhaust system is finished. The cockpit is completed and the instrument panel installed. The pedals are in place along with their connecting cables to the rear of the car. It is not long before the suspension elements, transmission, and engine cowling have been added and activity around the nearly completed car accelerates.

The many pieces finally come together and the crew can share a feeling of pride and accomplishment. After months of concentrated effort, what started as a gleam in the designer's eye roars to reality when the race car is started for the first time.

The car has been conceived and built to hug earth and yet to fly, but all assessments of its potential have so far been based on the success of quarter-scale models during wind tunnel runs. Actual performance will now be tested, modified, and further developed on the racetrack. Now, the human factor—the driver himself—is added to this new creation; his reactions, his skill, and his ability to relate the car's problems to the engineer come into play.

The driver will approach the car on the first day of testing with care and respect. Out on the track, at speed, it will be only the two of them. The car must not simply run, it must run fast. All the dreaming, all the computer readouts, all the dedication and labor and hopes of a whole team for a chance at winning: all this comes down, at first, to how fast the new car proves to be in the isolation of an empty speedway, witnessed only by its creators.

RITUALS

The race car, now with the paint and decals of the sponsor's livery, is loaded onto the team's specially outfitted, sixty-thousand-pound semi. Equipped with everything possibly needed for actual competition—including even a spare car—the big rig pulls out of the home shop days in advance of the first scheduled race meeting. Often, a grueling drive carries on through nighttime hours.

As dawn breaks, the crew's first task is unloading. At tracks with garages or canopies, the rigs are brought into the paddock area. At others, off-loading takes place right in the pits along the front straightaway.

The garage area on the morning of the first practice session is a scene of seeming chaos. Some cars are all but ready for the green light; others are in pieces. There is a sense of urgency. But small groups of racing people stop and chat, making the rounds on bikes, mopeds, or golf carts (usually used to tow cars to the fueling station or technical inspection area).

Officials, decked out in baseball-style caps with patches and embroidered shirts, have been on the scene since sunrise. Technical Committee members conduct inspections of the cars, ensuring compliance with the published rules and standards in order to keep things as fair and as safe as possible. Track inspections by the chief steward in the pace car and Safety Committee members in their crash rescue trucks continue until moments before practice begins.

In the Goodyear garage or tent, each team's tires are being mounted and balanced on their rims and prepared for the day's sessions. (Goodyear makes all the tires for all

competitors in this class of racing.) Tires must be specifically created for racing and approved by both the manufacturer and the racing association. According to Indy car rules, wheel diameter is restricted to fifteen inches and width to ten inches in front, fourteen inches on the rears. Unlike production tires designed to work on every type of road surface, race car tires are made to accommodate specific track conditions. A soft, sticky tire with no tread is needed to provide optimum cornering traction when running at high speed on oval tracks, where cars race only when the weather is dry. Different compounds are required for road-course use, and a specially grooved "rain tire" enables road competition in the wet. On the rim and ready to use, each tire weighs about forty pounds.

As the designated practice time approaches, a parade begins. Golf carts, loaded with tool boxes, air bottles, hoses, mounted tires, and even water coolers, begin towing the race cars from the paddock out to the pit lane.

The teams assemble around their cars in the pit area they have selected and set out the tools and equipment they will use all day. Signboards are placed at the racewall, which separates the track from the pit; beside each is an array of colored numbers.

Now, the drivers begin to wander out, conspicuous in their tight, one-piece driving suits and soft, formfitting shoes. Some socialize with other drivers, but many join their teams. Mostly, they just mark time.

Finally a green light signals that the track is open for practice. Some drivers are already sitting in their cars in anticipation, but for most this marks the beginning of final preparations. The competitors now don their head socks and helmets, taking time to survey the scene briefly while fastening their chin straps. Next, the gloves are pulled on and the areas between the fingers pressed down to get the fit just right. All the garments are fireproof.

How a driver readies himself as he approaches his car is as distinctive as his hair color or his sponsor's logo. His special signature could be a hop and a slide, a quickly measured step, or perhaps a casual foot on the car with a leg into the tub—the tightest fit in auto racing.

Once in, the driver is assisted by a crewman; the cockpit is so small that his five-point harness system must be connected for him and the shoulder straps tightened. The radio cord on his helmet is connected to another one in the car, and he's ready. He nods, and the motor is fired up.

Engine noise is heard from every direction, as each pit crew quickly gathers behind its car. Indy cars need a good push to get moving once in gear; it's all part of the procedure. One by one, they come out onto the pit lane, promenading slowly toward the track entrance. Some team members walk over to the racewall. Crew chiefs usually sport headsets for two-way radio communication with their drivers; all carry stopwatches and notebooks.

The first few laps are slow and are taken toward the inside of the track along the guardrail, to warm up the engine and oil for high-speed running.

Soon the cars advance to the fast portion of racing surface, known as "the groove." As speeds begin to climb

each crew gets ready to time the first "hot lap" of the day. As the race car comes down the front straightaway past a preselected point, watches are started and a timed lap is underway. All the hands holding watches are poised for the decisive moment when the car streaks by again. The time for one lap is registered as another is begun, and so the pattern continues. Each recorded time is displayed by the boardman for the driver to see on his next pass.

Practice running continues for a set number of laps or until a handling condition develops that requires a crew's immediate attention. As their car thunders down the pit lane toward them, crewmen take positions to guide the driver to a safe stop and begin a systematic appraisal of the car's life signs. Goodyear Tire engineers attack the car as soon as it stops, taking temperature readings from all four tires. One of the crew members attaches an air hose to the car and it rises up on its built-in air jacks so that tire diameters can be measured. These measurements are critical because the size of one tire relative to its mate on the other side, even down to a difference of one-eighth of an inch, can affect the car's performance.

While this is taking place, the crew chief and the team engineer bend down close to the cockpit and listen to the driver's analysis of the car's handling. Efforts to solve any problems begin immediately.

If the remedy requires a simple turn of a screw or even a spring change, a driver will often stay in the car. But if the weather is hot, not even the shade of a colorful umbrella held by one of the team will lower the temperature in the cockpit, so the driver will get out. Maybe he will stroll across the pit lane to lean on the racewall and get a better look at what everyone else is doing. If he has a mind to, he may put a stopwatch on his competition to see where he stands. When the work is completed, the head sock, helmet, and gloves go back on and he is belted into the car again. Once his car is started and pushed off, the driver resumes the quest for a quicker lap time.

In each pit, a different sequence of events takes shape. Success, progress, failure, sometimes total disaster: all happen as the day wears on. At short tracks the cars remain in the pits for all minor adjustments. For complete engine changes, they're pulled behind the pit wall where careful surgery may be performed out in the open regardless of the weather. But at big speedways, the garage offers refuge and some privacy. The golf carts run back and forth, their traffic directed by watchful officials.

After lunch, the business at hand in the Indy car pits revolves around "making the show." The hard work of the morning was all toward one end—to qualify with as quick a time as possible. There is a saying, "You can't win unless you get in," and the chances of being really competitive get better the farther up front you start the race.

At most Indy car events, qualifying is scheduled during two practice days and the qualifying sessions are conducted in the afternoons to insure that everyone has had an opportunity to get ready. At oval tracks, after the order of starting is determined by draw, the cars attempt to qualify one at a time; the fastest of two officially timed laps

is counted. At road courses, all the cars are permitted on the track during each session, with the fastest laps in either of those periods deciding the arrangement of the grid for race day.

The big exception to all of this is the Indianapolis 500. Indy is the biggest race in the world and it is orchestrated to milk every drop of drama possible from the hours, days, and weeks before the green flag is finally waved. The tremendous build-up—which often seems much longer than a month—is punctuated by two separate weekends of qualifying periods. Only the first-day qualifiers of the first weekend are eligible for the coveted "pole position"—the inside spot in the front row. In addition to gaining the advantage of starting on the pole, that driver wins a bonus. At Indy, a completed qualifying run consists of four consecutive laps, one car at a time, in front of crowds that rival those that will gather for race day. The speeds of the four laps are averaged. The order is determined by a

special draw. Each driver is allowed three qualifying runs, but to get "the pole" he must be the quickest on his first try.

There is little doubt that with the great importance "the pole" has at Indy, drivers who attempt to earn it come under a great deal of pressure. As various school bands parade past the grandstands, some drivers may be found sitting on the pit wall beside their cars as they go through "tech inspection"; some sit alone in their garages until the last minute. However they spend the time, they have a lot on their minds. Each realizes that piloting a speedway missile is something like driving a bullet—the aim has to be perfect. In this instance, it must be perfect during four laps with no excuses accepted.

Sitting in the car with the motor revving, waiting for his turn, the driver is very much on his own. If he is a good qualifier, he is reaching his peak mentally and everything is under control. He has already run every inch of his laps inside his head. The only things left are the uncontrollable variables—weather, track conditions, and car performance. Those he will handle with experience and savvy.

As soon as the car is pushed off, the crew chief leaves for the end of the racewall at the head of the straight where he will receive a green flag and a yellow flag from an official. During the second warm-up lap, the green flag is

waved to signal the chief starter that a qualifying attempt will begin. If at any time before the completion of the required four circuits the team is not satisfied with the car's performance, the yellow flag is used to "wave off" the run. In that case, except on a car's third attempt, the crew can push it to the end of the qualifying lineup and, if time permits, try again.

Regardless of the number of entries, only the thirty-three fastest cars are eligible for a position in the starting lineup at Indy. Many teams struggle through two qualifying attempts and still cannot achieve a competitive speed. On the final days, as the clock winds down, a large crowd usually forms around the push-off point to provide support for their favorites and watch the story unfold. Often there is more joy exhibited for earning a spot in the last row of the field than for the pole position itself.

There is sadness too. When a qualified car ceases to be one of the thirty-three fastest, it automatically is forced out of the lineup. For every driver who achieves his ambition to make the great race, there is one whose dream is shattered. The guy "sitting on the bubble" (the slowest of those who have completed qualifying runs) watches the last qualifying attempts like a man suspended in a world where time is frozen.

During the final practice session, race setups are perfected and the required number of tire sets are scuffed-in. But handling problems often continue to present themselves, and sometimes as the afternoon's running nears an end, the answers are far away. With their last laps completed, a few of the drivers relax for the first time all day. Others sit inside their cars and try to relate the difficulties they are still having to crews who listen intently. For some the situation cannot be improved and the dissatisfaction shows on their faces.

A migration back to the garage area begins when the cockpit conferences are completed. Race cars towed by golf carts along with firetrucks, tow-trucks, and mechanics pulling starter carts all move in procession. In the garages, the work continues. There is always something to do, as if it were sinful to declare oneself ready.

After qualifying for a five-hundred-mile race, many teams will remove a superfast "killer engine" and install a proven, reliable race motor. When they do so, the car is stripped down to the tub and the parts checked for structural failures. Then they are cleaned in solution, examined, and carefully reassembled to take on the stress of a long race. The garage area begins to look like the emergency room of a large metropolitan hospital, with bare tubs on rolling carts and gearboxes in pieces everywhere. Somehow, most of the teams always get things back together in plenty of time; others, though, will work long into the early-morning hours, and struggle all the way.

A different kind of activity goes on outside the security of the garage area, in the areas around the track. At Indy, the crowds become so large the night before the race that they take over the streets in riotous celebrations. The frivolity is in sharp contrast to the meticulous preparations going on inside the nearby garages.

THE CHASE

Crews arrive at the garage area as the first light illuminates their movement. The order of the hour is to get all necessary equipment out to the pit area before the public is let in and movement becomes a problem. But even as the loaded golf carts start moving, a growing number of credential-bearing media people and friends of the teams begin to congregate outside the open garage doors.

Lines of cars stretch for miles outside entrances to the infield. Once inside, they fill every available parking space, and fans press as close as possible to the safety fencing around the track. Reserved-ticket holders seeking out their seats and other early arrivals create spots of color in the grandstands.

The race cars are brought out into view, towed through an evergrowing throng to the fueling point. After certification, when their methanol fuel cells are filled and checked, they continue to their places along pit row. Marching-band music, majorettes, and crowds of race-day pilgrims all vie for attention in the arena where race cars gleam of chrome and freshly waxed paint. The confusion of motion is everywhere; there is even diversion in the sky as the Goodyear blimp circles majestically or several stunt planes perform. Some big sponsors, not wanting to miss a trick on this important morning, have brilliantly colored hot-air balloons tethered in strategic locations. You may catch a glimpse of the Electrolux tiger or the Budweiser team of Clydesdale horses on parade.

It has become the fashion for the large corporations that sponsor racing teams to entertain guests at races in protected enclaves of elegance; hospitality tents are set up near specially outfitted motor coaches in the paddock area. Here the privileged few prepare to watch the race. They may sample a five-course brunch complete with champagne and mingle with the driver and celebrities.

But the excitement of the hour soon entices them out along pit row, where crews are going through final drills. Some are spray-painting day-glo outlines on the pavement where tires will be placed and the race car will halt during the all-important pit stops in the race. While it is true that the fortunes of a team most often rest in the skill of their driver, there are occasions when the difference between victory and defeat comes down to pit work. To remain competitive, a crew must be able to change two tires and refill a forty-gallon fuel cell in under fifteen seconds. Mistakes in the pit can cause the loss of a race just as easily as a driver who puts a car into the wall on the last lap. Before a race, many pit crews go through dress rehearsals, while herds of onlookers scrutinize them.

Key officials keep the day on schedule much like the production staff of an epic movie. When it is time, each crew chief is directed to "grid" his car in its proper starting position. At Indy this lineup is done on the racing surface along the front straight; at other tracks, the pit lane is used. Once in position, each crew arranges its starting cart and other necessary gear around the car and gets set for a five-minute engine warm-up period.

An announcement calls the engines to life in unison for the first time since the last practice period. A crewman stands beside each car, flexing a spring-tensioned throttle control as each motor's voice rises, pops, then falls away, only to rise again in close rhythm with the others. It is now, surrounded by powerful roars from every direction, that one realizes the relative insignificance of all the pageantry up to this point. This dominant sound in the air refocuses attention on the essentials—the cars and their drivers. The challenge that awaits, the struggle to be first, is tinged with the seductive threat of death, and this hidden reality humbles all other concerns. Abruptly, silence falls, then the countdown continues.

The milling crowd grows with every minute, and it seems that the only thing preventing the race cars from being completely overrun is the protective cordon of the pit crews, standing guard in their colorful firesuits.

There is now a brief period of inactivity, but not relaxation. Crew chiefs stare at their cars; mechanics wonder if everything is right and think ahead to their tasks during pit stops. Some wander over to acquaintances standing nearby and joke about the crowd, but even their laughter is fraught with tension. Most know they have done everything possible to be ready, but they also know that something can go wrong in the blink of an eye, and each hopes it will not be the result of anything he overlooked.

The business of the day is almost at hand, and the drivers begin to appear, some escorted by beautiful women. They will spend the remaining minutes with their crews. Some drivers carefully tape tear-away shields on their helmet visors; some sit quietly on their cars after brief discussions with the team managers. Like a matador preparing to face a bull or a knight awaiting the joust, the driver now collects himself, turns inward, where his doubts and anxieties must be reconciled and put into perspective. If he is to win, he must believe he can.

Before long the national anthem has everyone at attention, and now the crowd turns toward the drivers dressing for the start. It is the same ritual seen during practice, but somehow different, more methodical. Once inside the car and with the buckling-up completed, each participant must handle the time left to him in his own way. The chief mechanic may huddle close by the driver and talk, or just scan the surroundings with him. It's almost showtime.

Someone passes the word: "Two minutes." The huddles break up. Pace cars are started and rotating lights begin flashing. Immediately, there are gestures of admiration and concern. Quickly, as if it breaks the rules of the game to show emotion, hands reach down to the cockpits; some momentarily rest on the driver's helmet or the edge of the windscreen, but others go for a gloved hand on the wheel. Not a shake so much as a touch, this shy public act—usually done without eye contact—reveals much.

The command is given: "Gentlemen, start your engines!"

At Indy, because of the cacophony, it is difficult to tell whether the motor of a specific car has turned over. You must observe the actions of the crews. The uproar of the crowd is so forceful that your attention is stolen from the cars and carried up into the surrounding grandstands, away from the teams now assembling at the rear wings to signal with arms high in the air that they are ready.

Sudden running motion recaptures your awareness as the men strain to launch their cars in ranks behind the pace cars, already moving toward the first turn.

With the field underway, crewmen dash back to their pits trailing their starting carts, and everyone settles into race position. Most prepare themselves in case their driver pits unexpectedly before the start. The race cars creep slowly round the track, weaving back and forth to scuff in tires, heating them up for better adhesion.

Soon the crowd is on its feet to wave hats or handkerchiefs as the field advances down the front straight for the first time. Many drivers wave back, making it seem as if the action were following a prepared script.

The script calls for another parade lap, after which all but one of the fancy pace cars pull off from the snaking formation and head for the safety of the pit lane. The remaining pace car increases the field's speed to about a hundred mph. Suddenly, with rooftop lights switched off, it too streaks for the pits and out of the way. The chief starter stands, green flags in hand, his headset crackling with the report, "Pace car pulling in…Starter, they're yours."

At the head of the front straightaway, the rows snap into place behind the pole car with all eyes riveted on the scene about to unfold. Suddenly the green is unfurled in a rapid flourish of cloth, and the cars fly past the line like a squadron of jet fighters. The chase is on.

When they break formation, it's every man for himself, a practice that has traditionally produced some hair-raising antics on the first lap. But if the start is safe, the pattern of cars begins its orderly grind through lead changes, challenges, and early dropouts. One car may limp back to the pits, or dart in for a simple handling adjustment, only to never make it out again. A driver may sit through long minutes of futile efforts from hands reaching everywhere at once, or simply switch off the engine, unbuckle, and get out. Whatever the scenario, the disappointed looks he gives the car as it is pushed behind the wall are always the

same…the damn thing let him down. The crew then is left with cleaning everything out of their area even as the race goes on around them.

As the laps mount steadily toward a predetermined pit stop, the helmeted and goggled "bugmen" stand by patiently. Protective coverings rob the fuelers of their real identities so most have a name embroidered somewhere in plain sight. Fueling demands that two crewmen work in close harmony, because if anything goes wrong the results can be catastrophic. One man maneuvers a large gravity-fed filler hose and another is responsible for catching any overflow with a narrower vent hose. Both hoses are connected to the team's fuel supply stored in a free-standing metal tank in their area. The hose nozzles must be properly engaged to the car's filler couplings; otherwise a pressurized spray of highly flammable methanol could engulf the driver and crew. A malfunction of the coupling apparatus at the end of either hose would be equally hazardous. Fire extinguishers and buckets of water line the inside of the pit wall.

Only seven team members are permitted over that wall during any stop. One is the driver, of course; another is the boardman who signals him with lap times throughout the race and is positioned out next to the track. Subtract the two fuelers and that leaves three tire changers. One takes care of the front tires and makes wing adjustments. He also signals the driver when the pit stop work is completed. Two others perform duties at the rear of the car and handle the push-off. The fueler handling the vent hose also wields an air hose. When the car rolls in, he connects this hose to a special coupling linked to on-board pneumatic jacks that automatically raises the car so that tire work can be done; when the work is finished, he pulls this hose free and the car drops to the ground.

A well-drilled crew anticipates an opportunity to conduct its precision ballet about every seventy miles of accident-free ("green light") racing, but they are constantly alert in case the yellow caution flag comes out, enabling their car to make an unscheduled stop.

Every so often, the evil spectre that haunts this sport grabs everyone and shakes the hell out of them. To be in racing is to understand the meaning of uncertainty and the presence of danger. There is always the possibility of a major disabling injury, or worse. For most participants, the only cost of success at this level of competition is years of hard work, large quantities of talent, and a big dose of luck. For some, the luck will run out, and the price extracted is much higher.

Official observers stationed around the course will radio that a car is in trouble even before it comes to rest. Two of the men who get the news first are sitting in the main crash rescue truck with the motor running: the safety chief, a trained paramedic, and his medical director, a doctor specializing in critical care medicine. The report, "Yellow, yellow, yellow!" interrupts them and a sense of urgency fills the vehicle, immediately on its way toward the crash site. Additional reports tell the physician how severe things appear to be, and the two men begin shouting their

33

directions for the handling of various aspects of the emergency. These are professionals saving precious seconds by getting things organized en route. Both know the drivers in this race not only by name and comprehensive medical records, but often through binding friendships with them and their families. This is a job of the heart as much as the conscience, and it shows.

Once the threat of fire has been eliminated, the medical men turn their attention to a patient who may be pale, bleeding, or gasping for air, his blood pressure plummeting. Although they act aggressively and decisively only seconds after the devastation, the strain on their faces reveals that they care deeply. Each knows that his life-saving skills are counted on, not only by the driver who lies in the stillness of the wreckage, but also by the others who drive by the scene in procession behind the pace car.

No two accidents are ever exactly the same. Sometimes there has been only a spin and no contact with the wall, so a friendly tow is all that is required. The crash truck usually arrives to find the driver already out of the disabled car and walking away. Though merely shaken up, with perhaps some bruises from being thrown around, he will be stopped and checked over for signs of anything more serious as a matter of policy.

After the driver is seen to, the safety director begins to supervise the clean-up. In hardly any time at all, the car is hoisted by a wrecker and carried back to its crew. Then a group of eager sweepers goes over the crash area to satisfy the director's trained eyes looking for nuts, bolts, and slivers of metal. After a final inspection, the official vehicles head back to their stations and notify Race Control that the track is ready for competition to resume.

PARTICIPANT PARKING
SEPTEMBER 22-23, 1978   Nº   044

Very little distance is given up to pursuers if a driver can use caution periods to make required stops. Teams getting good mileage will try to wait for these opportunities rather than call their cars in under green conditions. At the first indication of a yellow light, each pit becomes a close-order drill. A driver approaching the pit entrance will come right in, so his crew must be ready. It is still important to complete the stop and get back out quickly, because passing is prohibited under a yellow. Thus the closer to the pace car a driver rejoins the pack, the better his situation when there is a "restart."

At a time like this the pit lane resembles a cross between a freeway during rush hour and a drag strip. Front-tire men from each team are out near the traffic, waving like hell to attract the attention of their pilot bearing down on them. Movement of the bugmen, who are crouched and waiting anxiously, is limited by the length of the refuel-

ing hoses, so the final approach must be within the outlines painted earlier in the day. This is accomplished with a target on a pole held from behind the pit wall and marking exactly where the nose of the car should come to rest.

Pressure is what the pit stop is all about, mostly the pressure to do it well, which translates to fast. As the cars storm in, crewmen test-fire unwieldy pistol-shaped wrenches and check the yards of air hose trailing along behind them. When the driver stops on the mark, he begins revving the motor to prevent it from stalling, and this constant pulsing becomes a cadence for the specialists who are now attaching fuel nozzles and encircling the car with rubber hosing.

Jacks appear below the car and force it upward as the kneeling tire men already have their impact wrenches undoing wheel nuts. It seems that the spindly fingers just finish extending when the old rubber is pulled free of the hubs and a new pair is slapped into place.

Triggers on the wrenches are pulled again and a "rat-tat-tat" of simulated machine-gun fire accompanies the eccentric wobbling of used wheels dropped hastily on the pavement. Even in this maelstrom there are pockets of quiet grace, as if another game were being played. His tire change completed early, the front man takes off like a quarterback on a roll-out, confidently slinging an air hose out of harm's way and passing his cumbersome instrument to a receiver over the pit wall. Returning to his position at the outside edge of the pit, he surveys similar broken-field running by the rear-tire men, who then form up behind the car, waiting for the bugmen to make a move.

The driver sits impatiently throughout these proceedings, a captive staring at the outstretched hand of a crewman telling him it's not over yet. He doesn't have long to wait though.

Crewmen behind the wall watch the level in a hand-made gauge on the fuel tank as it inches closer to a plotted line. When that mark is reached, indicating that a full load has been passed to the car, a "deadman" lever is released, cutting off any flow through the main hose.

By now the vent man can see bubbles through a clear section of hose in front of him. That signals both bugmen to pull away, the fuel man first. The hose to the jacks is yanked as they leave, lowering the refueled, re-tired car in a loud rush of escaping air. With his gearbox already engaged before the full weight of the car can be felt by the suspension, the driver begins applying power as soon as he has rubber on the ground, coordinating with the send-off from the rear. The two men back there in the acrid exhaust fumes have been poised for endless seconds, and now, finally, they expel their energy in a rush of limbs and color that whizzes by and takes your breath away. In an assault of wailing turbocharger noise, and as wildly spinning tires claw the ground, the push-off men keep going. Their grimacing faces reveal that every ounce of force is being delivered to the trailing edge of the rear wing, which suddenly no longer needs them, and so forsakes their helpful hands to run alone.

Returning triumphantly, crewmen pass used tires behind the pit wall and climb over, relieved that this time it went as planned. One measures tire diameters and checks the condition of the rubber, while the bugmen rescale the wall, doing what looks like a vaudeville snake dance with the fueling hoses. Their contortions ensure that fuel trapped in the hosing is poured back into the tank for an accurate accounting of the rate of consumption.

Visible across the track, above the brightly painted helmets in the pits, a wisp of green is being waved at fence level, indicating a restart. During a yellow the warriors bunch up tight behind the pace car, so that when they are let loose to soar again, the drivers are all treated to combat as fresh as the initial encounter of the day, hours earlier. Fans sometimes lose a bit of interest when a leader puts a considerable distance between himself and close rivals, thereby apparently reducing the number of duels to be engaged. They may fail to appreciate the artistry it takes to hold a large lead—the concentration of effort and energy—especially in late stages of a race.

But now, in the closing laps and after a yellow, the odds have been evened out, and the fans will get what they came to see—savage wheel whisking that eats up roadway at an amazing velocity. It is now, when a quick group is running headstrong and hellbent together, gulping down large quantities of straightaway, that the observer just might truly comprehend how fast these cars are going. Each driver is at the fringes of his car's performance—a speed of 290 feet per second—yet each is still taking shots at the others going into every turn. One tries a lunge to the inside, and his target blocks him with a lightning response that removes any advantage: the best of the breed are going at it, hammer and tongs.

In the pits, engineers are busy with calculators hoping to reassure team managers that their drivers have enough fuel to make it to the finish. Here, the results of the race may be read in silent decimals on liquid crystal readouts. But on the track where the job is getting done, the drivers fight tired neck muscles and mental strain in a hectic environment of high temperatures and punishing vibrations. Mileage figures mean nothing to them now.

For spectators safe in their seats, the warfare is enjoyable, vicarious. Favored competitors are engaged in a powerful game of dominance and courage on an unforgiving stage. Down there on the field of battle, though, there is something of a higher order going on.

Those in the thick of it believe all this has a meaningful purpose. It takes more than the promise of a paycheck to encourage their participation. For those who grip steering wheels behind tiny windscreens, a call to excellence and an inner discipline enable them to rise above the encroaching violence only inches outside their speeding cocoons. Each performs despite the constant threat. Only winning will define their glory, their status, their acceptance. For all this and more, they keep taking those heart-stopping chances.

by Chet Jezierski

PART **1** BIRTH

THE CONCEPT MODEL

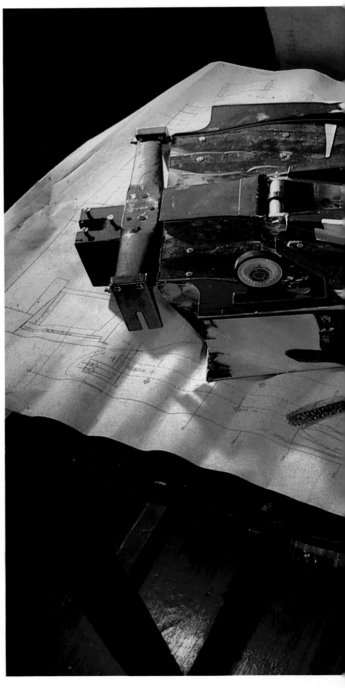

Above: Eric Broadley, Designer and Managing Director of Lola Cars Ltd., studies a quarter-scale driver cut-out used in creating a model of the "short-track" version of the T-800 Indy Car.

Mario Andretti, Driver:

A Championship car like a Formula One is an absolute thoroughbred. There's no compromise to anything. It's designed to the limits of the rules and for one purpose only: to go very fast, do it efficiently, with nothing to spare.

Nigel Bennett, Designer:

I don't think I'm particularly original. I don't think I have that kind of ability, and I've met very few people who have. Possibly Colin Chapman is the only guy I ever worked with who has thought things up from basic principles. Most of it is evolution. Brilliant ideas usually come in totally new areas, and this form of racing is nothing really very new. So it's just a case of improving on what you've got, looking at the problem areas and working past them. I can't remember having any lightning strikes recently.

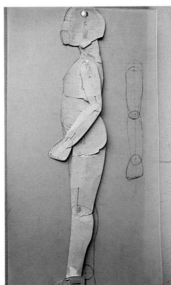

Right: The wooden model—minus cowlings, wings, and wheels—rests on a workbench along with tools and materials used to modify its shape during wind-tunnel tests. One of many interchangeable underbody elements, carefully drilled with numerous pressure holes, can be seen at far right.

Tony Cicale, Development Engineer:

You go to the wind tunnel with a basic quarter-scale model about forty-five inches long and twenty inches wide, which has pressure sensors on all the bottom surfaces, wings, and top surface areas. It's built so you can substitute a variety of test pieces for the standard ones, so you also take along your odd assortments of tape, plaster, and everything else that you would use to modify the model quickly—hacksaws and drills and things like that. You view those modifications in the window, and the things that look promising you incorporate into the design of the car.

THE WIND-TUNNEL EXPERIMENTS

Robin Herd, *Designer:*

A race car is only doing three things. It's either accelerating, braking, or cornering. I always approach this systematically. You break the acceleration down into high power, low weight, low drag, and good traction. Then you break each one of those four down into various subfactors and analyze each one to see where you can get a potential gain. Braking is not particularly important in racing, but in cornering, you need grip. This results from a high coefficient to tire friction and a lot of aerodynamic downforce.

The carefully shaped, plastic and wooden underbody element is designed for quick substitution with a similar structure on the main model. Spaghetti-like tubing transmits surface pressure readings.

Tony Cicale:

We have a "moving ground" at Imperial College, which removes the boundary layer of air that gets built up by the normal circulation of air in the tank. You do that because there's no known boundary layer on actual ground surfaces. So in order to simulate actual conditions as realistically as possible, we try to remove that boundary layer with a belt that rotates at the same speed as the air passing over the model, about forty-three mph. The model hangs over this "moving-ground belt," but the wheels are not connected to the model or the suspension components. They are hung independently, from the stationary floor of the tunnel, and rotate on their own axles. The model itself is supported overhead by a "balance arrangement" that can measure the vertical and longitudinal forces generated on it. We can't measure changes made to the model that affect the wheels. That's a problem in this type of tunnel. The way around that would be to mount the wheels directly on the model, but have them somehow slide up and down in the chassis. The model has to be free to move up and down so that the overhead balance can measure the loads.

Gordon Coppuck, Designer:

The wind tunnel gives us three numbers: the downforce on the front wheels, the downforce on the rear wheels, and the drag of the car. After that, it's up to us, but it gives us those numbers and as a designer I have to use them in whatever way I can. Most of us now run pressure probes, probably a couple of dozen at a time, and they record where the high and low pressures are on the model and their magnitude. From that you can put together an accurate picture of how the air is flowing.

Patrick Head, Designer:

The tunnel we use has a working section of four by five feet, so you want to use a model as large as you can because that gets you as close to a similar situation with the real car. You don't want to get into a size where you actually get wall effects. Then the air flow over the model is being affected by its proximity to the walls of the tunnel. In a four-by-five-foot working section, a quarter-scale model is just right for a race car.

The race car engineer who conceived the Lola T-800 Indy Car, Nigel Bennett, along with Mark Williams, also of Lola, and Tony Cicale of Newman/Haas prepare an assembled model for testing inside the Imperial College wind tunnel.

Tony Cicale:

The model is built primarily out of bass wood or mahogany. The bass wood doesn't have any knots in it, it's easy to shape the contoured surfaces, and you can screw into it and hammer on it a little bit. You're able to machine it, because you can saw without cracking or rupturing. It's just a nice modeling wood. We also use aluminum and Lexan [clear plastic] to make most of the flat pieces or the shaped, curved pieces.

Overleaf: The model is suspended by a control pylon (*right*) and support rod above a moving-ground belt during a three-minute run in the wind tunnel.

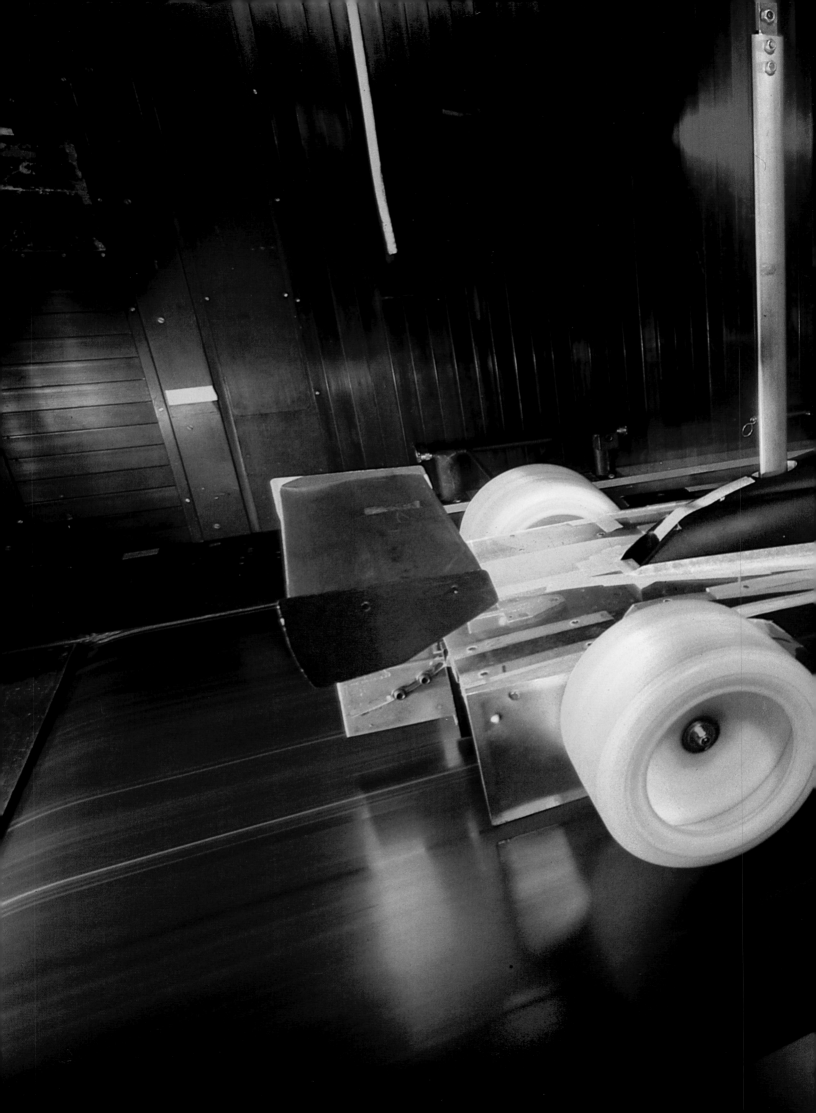

Above: Deep inside the model, a "scani-valve" collects pressure readings and feeds them up through the support pylon and out to the computer monitor. At the completion of each run, the engineers pore over the data and evaluate the potential of the model elements. Following months of such sessions, the best combinations are incorporated into hundreds of drawings for the full-scale race car.

Geoff Ferris, Designer:

Particularly with ground-effect cars you have to worry about the structure that holds the sidepods on. We've had them rip away from underneath the car with the suction effect. Also, the areas around the cockpit distort considerably at high speed. We noticed it and found that with the PC-6 and the PC-7 the drivers were saying the cockpit enclosure was pressing on their hands when they were traveling at high speed. When we watched the car in the wind tunnel, we could see the whole of the cockpit cave in and really take a quite different shape from the original design.

Tony Cicale:

I don't mind any regulation, as long as they didn't spring it on you, and gave you enough time to think about it—design around it and test around it. Basically, time is the only parameter. Restrictions aren't really a problem. Everyone has them.

Nigel Bennett:

There's a considerable gap under the sidepod, and so it isn't a two-dimensional flow problem any longer. The flow comes out at one place from under the pod and rushes back into the other side. The pattern becomes extremely complicated, and the trick is to use that flow to get energy into the air already in the tunnels. It's not just a lump rushing through a Venturi, and following Bernoulli's theory. It's complicated by air rushing in from the side and forming a very powerful vortex. Now, we have a three-dimensional flow, and the shape of the pod underneath is governed by what happens outside.

DECISIONS AND DRAWINGS

John Barnard, Designer:

You always come back to the thing we're all striving for and that's minimum drag with maximum downforce, or, in other words, the relationship of drag to downforce efficiency. This is one of the areas that the ground-effect cars have improved. There used to be a lot of people saying it would never work on a Champ car because there's too much drag. But it's only a case of being able to tune the amount of downforce you get from the ground effect to the scale you want, and thereby reduce the drag.

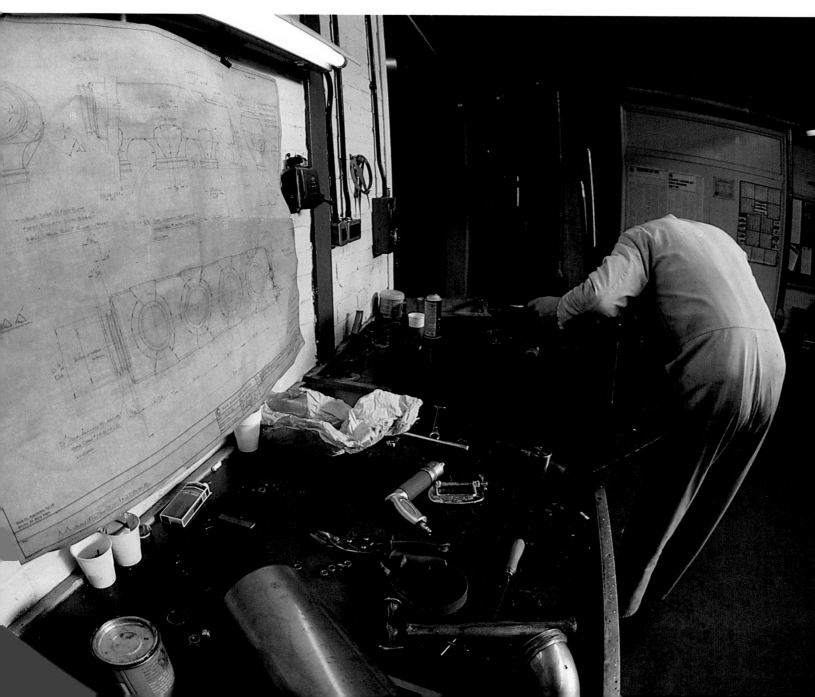

BUILDING BEGINS

Nigel Bennett:

Designing a car is not very pleasant, in terms of sheer hours to get the job done. It's about six hundred drawings. I started on the Lola T-800 in October, which was too late, and worked between sixty and eighty-five hours every week until the thing began running. Four days off for Christmas and that was it. Every time I do that, which has only been a couple of times, I swear I'll never do it again. It's just not enjoyable. You have to be sure it's going to be worth it in the end.

Keith Duckworth, Engine Designer:

Aerodynamics of cars are obviously going to be more important than engines. I think that engines were basically the same during the period before Chapman invented his Venturi car, that the cars were very competitive because they'd all sorted out the utilization of weight and general aerodynamics, and we had a lot of cars that were all running the same speed. Then Chapman made his great breakthrough and that rewrote the whole book. Now if the engines remain the same, obviously the plus or minus three percent change in power advantage available becomes terribly insignificant and the exploitation of aerodynamics is the thing. There's an awful lot of meaningless testing of engines when actually the important factor of the Indianapolis scene is the design of the cars and the aerodynamics of the cars. But people don't seem to be able to recognize that. They all would rather play around with engines than sort out aerodynamics and handling, and therefore we have a great lot of engine meddlers. Aerodynamic changes and ground effect are worth things like a hundred horsepower and to get that by meddling around with engines, once you fix your boost and a few other things, just isn't possible. Therefore, the effort is, in fact, going in the wrong direction.

A full-scale wooden "buck" (*below*) is used to create a mold for a cockpit enclosure (*opposite, above left*). Other builders begin the tedious process of scribing the outlines of major chassis components on sheets of aluminum.

John Barnard:

After a few decisions on what sort of wheel base and track, I'd spend two months doing a quarter-scale layout, which is sort of a basic plan. Starting more or less with four wheels and a piece of paper, I connect them with the chassis and the engine and so on. You obviously design around that lump in the back because apart from the driver, which is sort of a fixed thing, everything else is fairly fluid. So, you've got the driver and then whatever engine you've been given to design around. I mean, even the gearbox now is a fairly fluid piece inasmuch as you can do your own case without too much problem. To actually get all the drawings done even with an assistant takes me nearly five months. I try and draw every nut and bolt on the car. I like to get it all on paper. That's one of my big things, if you like, to have it drawn as much as I can before anybody puts a hammer to metal. I reckon if I can't draw it, then the fabricator's going to have a helluva time making it. There are one or two exceptions like exhaust pipes where I've drawn enough of them, or have enough of an idea where they're going to run, that I can allow ample room for them. I wouldn't go in and detail every pipe. But, just about everything else I like to put down on paper. You get to a point where everything's fixed enough that you can then start parceling drawings out to be made. But during that time, you're having the basic stuff made while you're finishing off all the details.

Jim Hall, Team Manager:

The rules are made and that's either the maximum or the minimum or some number that defines the category of the race car. "Stretching it" is running outside of the rules as far as I'm concerned, and I don't have any interest in doing that. I feel that whatever they are, we should all compete on the basis of their guidelines, and they should be well enforced so I don't have to concern myself about other people trying to stretch them. I think in order to be a successful competitor and be comfortable with what you're doing, you have to feel everybody runs under the same regulations, otherwise it's a joke.

Nigel Bennett:

To accomplish the carbon fiber work on the chassis, first you build a full-size wood and plaster buck, rubbed down until you have a life-size of exactly what you want. You get the carbon fiber in a cloth form just like you buy a roll of fiberglass. And there are two ways of doing the process: it's either done by "prepreg" or a "wet lay-up," the "prepreg" being the better way. You buy the cloth impregnated with a resin that only cures with heat, and so you must store the cloth in a refrigerator. When you're ready, you lay it into a mold produced from the buck, and the outer layer is cured under pressure and heat. Then aluminum honeycomb is laid in, followed by the inner skin, and it's cured again. So you finish up with a sandwich. If it's done with a "wet lay-up," as soon as you brush the resin in it's starting to cure and you've got a limited amount of time to play with it. That's generally a more laborious method of doing it. The finished product is very strong, but unfortunately very brittle. So you've got to be a little bit careful how you use it. It will absorb an enormous amount of energy and not deform. It's a bit like glass. It doesn't bend, but it breaks.

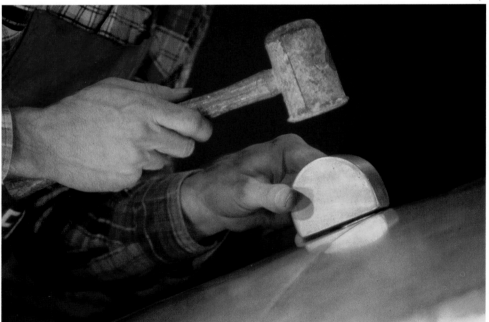

A fabricator bends
around a jig (*top left*)
bulkhead pieces, whi
drilled for riveting an
other elements of th
(*above right*) to form
sembly.

Gordon Coppuck:

The most rewarding part of being involved in the design of a racing car is that you draw it and see it absolutely as quickly as humanly possible. But if you haven't got any idea of roughly what you want, you're not going to be a designer for very long. You've got to be able to give the fabricator an idea of what it is, even if you haven't got a proper drawing. If it's something that's slightly difficult, you might start off with a sketch, make two or three attempts, then finally produce an engineering drawing. I prefer to have engineering drawings of almost the whole car.

Jackie Howerton, Builder:

You make a fixture called a "jig" that has the shape of the drawing and then form the aluminum around it just like a mold. That way, each piece you make off that fixture is exactly the same. Had you made that piece by hand, it would probably be all right the first time, but the next one would be a problem. You couldn't interchange the parts.

THE TUB
TAKES FORM

Jackie Howerton:

You've got a tub that's eight feet long with different pieces attached to it—front bulkhead, your dash bulkhead, the front arm pick-ups, seat and seat back, the roll bar, and so forth. They've all got to be real accurate, and you must have somewhere to go to make sure these things are in the right place with respect to the drawings. So we start off with a rigid table similar to a "surface plate" in a machine shop; this guarantees the accuracy of your tub. And that's one of the things you have to have in this business, because there are places on these cars where the accuracy is in thousandths of an inch. So you've got to have a table that's pretty accurate. We built one especially for this job. I think it's pretty much common sheet-metal practice on the tub, insofar as the inner skin and so forth have several angles to them. When you do aluminum body work that gets pretty tricky. That's really more like art work than it is sheet-metal work.

Richard Fried, Mechanic:

I think about trying to put the car together so it's safe. I don't want the guy to get hurt, so I try not to do anything negligently. Nobody does. If you see any Mickey Mouse stuff, you want to fix it. Sometimes you get into a lot of fault-finding with people trying to pin the blame on anybody. A lot of guys will never admit they made a mistake. That's not being honest with yourself.

Al Unser, Sr., Driver:

Before he did the drawings, the designer wanted to know how tall I was, leg length and all that. I gave all that to him, and after that I couldn't care less. He says, "You like certain things?" I told him I want the gear shift far enough away from me and stuff like that, that's all. I'm not too picky.

Rick Mears, Driver:

A car always tells you something when you get in it. And all cars are different. You can build two that are identical, and they will both feel different in little ways. It's just like wearing a favorite pair of shoes. You've worn them for five years and they feel good and comfortable. You put on another pair, and they just feel strange. But when you wear that new pair for about thirty minutes, they start feeling like home again. That's the same way a car feels when you first get in it. Even though you sat in it in the garage and had the seat made to fit, the steering wheel where you want it, the pedals put where you want them, and all the pads where you want them, it just doesn't feel the same. Even though you've done the best you can do sitting still in the garage, when you go out on the track, the car feels different again. Until you drive it for a while. Then it starts getting comfortable, and you feel accustomed to it.

Above: "Cleeko" fasteners and special pliers hold tub components in place atop the fabrication table, littered with tools and cardboard patterns. *Right:* Al Unser, Sr., checks the fit of his new car with the builder, Jackie Howerton.

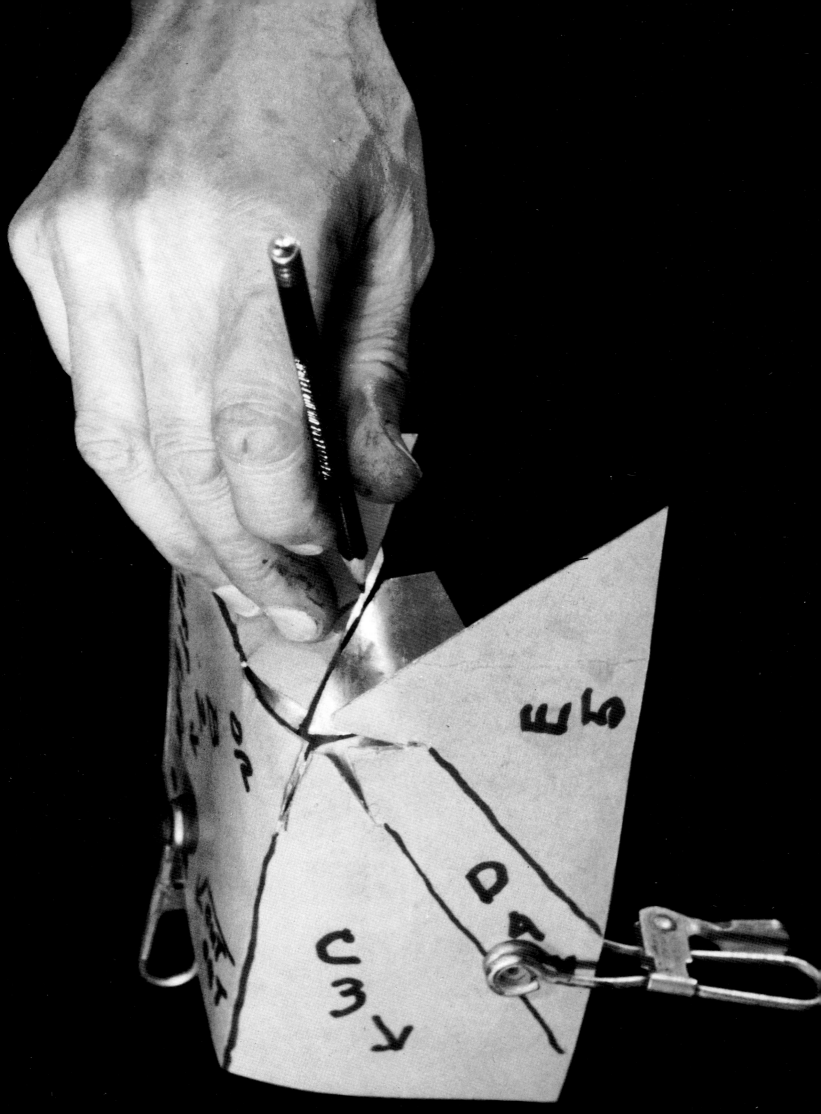

Jackie Howerton:

You sit there and try to figure out how you're going to get the metal to fit the shape and even with a ball or sphere, if you make enough segments, you can make something flat very round—just with a bunch of flat strips. When there's no tooling or anything to bend this aluminum into shape, you lay it out with a pencil or scribed line in little teeny increments. On some bends you might have maybe thirty or forty teeny bends. You start at zero on one end, and you go out to how wide this shape is gonna be. Then you fill it with these little bitty lines from zero and you just keep going over and over and over, and on one end you'll have maybe thirty or forty lines laid out on the sheet metal. On the other end, they all come to the same point. It's just a big long cone laid out on there. So you bend each one of those a couple of degrees. To the human eye it looks like you put it in some type of special shape guide and just bent it around.

Tony Cicale:

Someone is going to get credit for an innovation whether he deserves it or not. Colin Chapman certainly capitalized on ground effects, as did Patrick Head, and you can ask ten different people and get seven different answers as to who invented it. The fact of the matter is, ground effects was well known for some time, although it wasn't well understood. About fifteen years ago Ford and Chevrolet investigated in that area, along with a host of graduate students from various universities. Looking through reams of SAE papers back in the time when Chapman was doing work, there was someone at MIT who did a paper for Lotus on ground-effect cars. In fact they even built a cart and did a lot of theoretical evaluations on this cart that constituted their "moving ground wind tunnel." We still have that cart at Cornell University. So one person may get the credit for the revolution, because he was the one who put the whole package together. But he certainly didn't "invent" it. There were many people involved, and I think it's certainly wrong to give one person credit for any breakthrough of those proportions.

Colin Chapman, Designer:

I like to innovate because really that is *the* major part of motor racing that interests me: the design and the innovation of the cars. Motor racing goes through periods when there is very little innovation, when it's just a question of everybody producing virtually the same car or copies of the innovators', and the innovators haven't come up with any ideas over a reasonable period of time. Then the design tends to stagnate. When this occurs motor racing comes down to preparation and very minute changes and who has lots of resources. The people who've got the most cars and the most engines are the people who are going to succeed. And, of course, the drivers who can drive just that little bit better. That doesn't have the interest for me that motor racing does at the moment when innovation has sort of taken off again and there's a whole new, fresh field of experimentation to go through.

Patrick Head:

I have food on the table, and I amuse myself. Really, that's it. I mean I don't conceptualize or think about it to the point of what I'm achieving. I'd much rather be doing what I'm doing than designing washing machines. I don't really feel that people sitting down and designing a washing machine with one more orange knob on it that gives an extra jiggle to the clothes and gets a whiter wash are doing anything more productive than I am. I'm not looking to judge the worth of what we do. I'm here, there's a market for it, we can find money to do it. And that's enough, you know. The alternatives as an engineer are not necessarily any more worthwhile, and I would doubt there are very many that are more varied and more interesting.

Jackie Howerton:

I was pretty charged up and really proud of the tub. I even made sure that all the aluminum parts on it were not scratched during construction. They were all handled as easily as we could, so when we had the finished product, it looked like something that came out of an airplane factory or what have you. I don't remember anyone looking at that tub who wasn't impressed with it.

Overleaf: The finished tub following gluing and riveting.

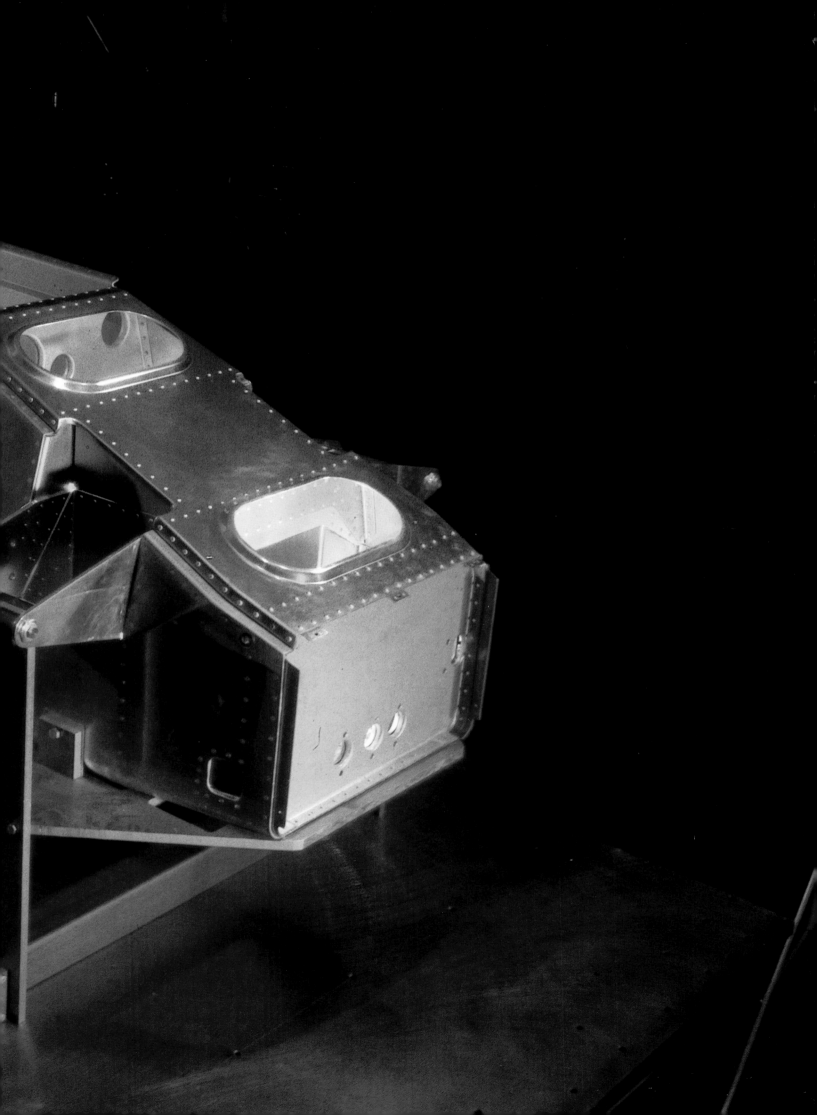

George Heuning, Crew Chief:

This is what I do all year long. It's a full-time profession. You wouldn't believe the hours we work. We don't punch time-clocks. We're a bunch of gypsies, and I don't think I could work a job where I had to punch a timeclock. But that has its advantages and disadvantages too. If I got paid by the hour, I'd be a rich man. The average person—forty hours a week, five days a week, figure a two-week vacation—works two thousand hours a year. I work somewhere in the vicinity of four thousand, eight hundred hours in one year. I'm not complaining, mind you. If I don't like it, there's the door. Once in a while you say, "What the hell am I doing here? What's it gettin' me?" It's not unusual for us to work seven days a week all through the wintertime too. Most people think that come wintertime, hell, you just kick back and don't do anything. We tire test. Build cars. There's a lot more involved than a lot of people realize.

Keith Duckworth:

Because of the long time it takes to manufacture most of the pieces and the uncertainty of the market, along with the use of a lot of precision machine tools, we decided that we must adopt a policy of asking people in advance whether they are interested in buying an engine, with a view to trying to get a firm order, and asking for a twenty-five-percent deposit six months before we would deliver. By circularizing all the people who were likely to be interested in having engines, we would then be able to get a batch together. We would decide it would be suitable for us to try and manufacture a batch of engines for May or January next year, and then about seven or eight months before it, we would circularize people to find out how many engines they would like on that January date and get firm orders accompanied by deposit. They are not exactly off-the-shelf things and it's unlikely that casual customers would come in and just buy a DFX [Cosworth's Indy car engine]. You would expect the majority of teams who compete in high levels of motor racing to be able to plan the six months ahead as they need that kind of time to build a car or find a car to suit the engine, because the car and engine tend to be, for a successful team, very much of a package. The car virtually needs to be designed for the engine, especially as the engine in our case forms the total part of the structural connection between the rear wheels and the tub the driver sits in.

Colin Chapman:

Since motor cars have been built, particularly racing cars, the emphasis has been on streamlining. It was realized that a racing car would go faster if it created a minimum of disturbance to the air it was passing through, so racing cars had streamlined bodies. Everybody was concerned with the reduction of drag to enhance the maximum speed. But any streamlined shape with air flowing over it creates lift. So these streamlined bodies were in fact tending to lift the car off the road at speed. In fact, they were certainly reducing the contact pressure between the tire and the ground, but this was hardly understood at the time. Then we suddenly realized that the next avenue to explore was not only to reduce the drag, but to reduce the drag in such a way that it did not increase lift. In fact, we got to the point where it was beneficial to counteract the lift by putting negative lifting surfaces on the car—wings and aerofoils. We started off with a crude sort of spoilers and "flips" up the back, and we realized that it was worth putting an actual aerofoil on the front to hold the nose down and on the back to hold the tail down. The increase in lap time due to the added aerodynamic weight on the car gave a greater increase in performance than a loss of performance due to the aerodynamic drag created by these extra wings. And so that was a ten-year era where we decided that wings were a big thing and drag was less important. What was more important was down load or "negative lift." The whole "ground effect" thing came about as I sat there thinking, "Well, this seems odd to me that we have a car body that fundamentally must produce lift and drag, and to counteract that lift, we have to put aerofoils on the car to produce negative lift, which also produced drag." So there we were with two vertical forces canceling each other out, creating lots of drag in order to cancel out the vertical forces. Now, this is crazy. We should find a way of producing negative lift without attendant drag, and so I thought, "Let's make air flow under the car instead of just flow over it." Up to then, of course, people had always ignored the underside of a car. If you look at a normal car, it's all chassis girders and exhaust pipes and junk. The car aerodynamics that had been done in a wind tunnel were really based on aircraft, and of course an aircraft doesn't fly six inches off the ground, so the science of aerodynamics was barely applicable to motor vehicles. That was really what I started to do. I said, "If we can make air flow under the car, it can flow through a divergent duct rather than on the Venturi principle, such that it will produce negative lift to counteract the positive lift, without increasing the drag. We will then have a significant gain in performance."

THE ENGINE BLOCK
IS CARVED BY COSWORTH

Keith Duckworth:

The DFX is a fairly conventional V-8 made with all aluminum castings for the main structure and magnesium for the cam covers. The water pumps, which suffer badly from corrosion with magnesium, are also in aluminum, as are parts of oil pumps, because it simplifies the design. The hardware is very conventional. The crank shaft is made of a very good alloy steel and nitrited, and so are our con rods. We've got virtually no titanium in the engine, and very few plastic parts. We do not use things like aluminum con rods because the life of those at the speeds we run at is inadequate. Bearings and many other parts are in conventional metals. But things like valve springs tend to be fairly exotic. And the gear train that drives the cam shaft is all vac remelted, very high alloy steel—and all its teeth are ground rather than cast.

58

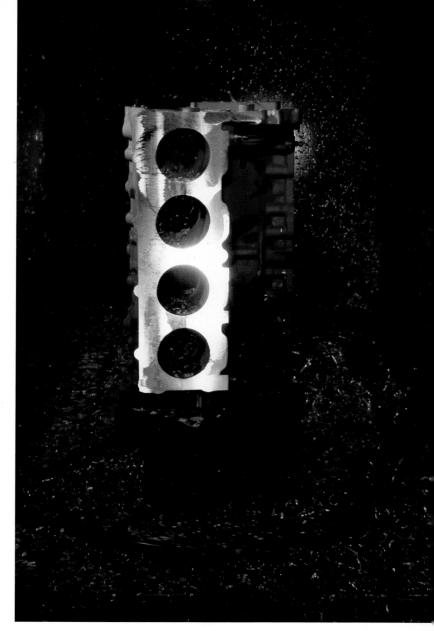

Keith Duckworth:

We were fairly early into numerically controlled machining as our output grew, especially when we saw that to stay in Indianapolis racing we had to increase production. That capacity arrived with two machining centers for making the blocks and heads needed to get a big output in the market. This "computer numerical control" uses programming, permits easier changes of program, and has advantages over tape. It runs the cycles and automatically changes the tool that's used on the machining centers, all without being touched. You program and record the memory of a work cycle, and you can run that program back through a tape printer to produce a piece of tape. Then, when you use the operator for something else, you can recover the memory from the tape.

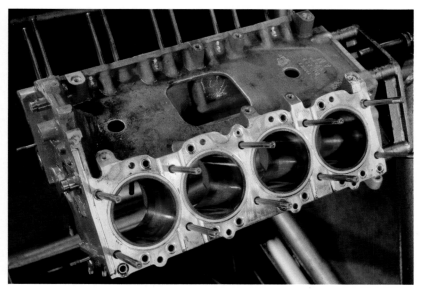

Far left: A Cosworth technician watches a multi-headed cluster tool inch toward the cast-aluminum engine block to begin a series of automated machining processes. With the grinding completed (*above*), the DFX will soon undergo many additional refinements on its way to the final assembly area. *Left:* The finished product.

Keith Duckworth:

It takes six months to build one...roughly. But we wouldn't build the one, would we? We would wait till we've got enough orders to justify making a batch. Obviously we have blocks and other things that are going through in continuous numbers, the spares, you know. I should think that we could generally build an engine in a fortnight, because we're bound to have one set of bits, and to actually assemble it, it takes a week. A fortnight, I suppose, to safely build and test it.

DROP-FORGING PISTONS

Keith Duckworth:

For the performance levels of most racing around the world, you need a forged piston rather than a die cast piston that production cars have. When we found that we couldn't get supplies, we bought a five-hundred-ton forging press to forge our own pistons. We forge them from bar stock and complete the machining here. This is "flow-forming." You just take a slug of metal from a bar or cylindrical piece, cut off the right volume, and put it down in the bottom of a die as a solid lump when it's at about 500°C. The hole is the shape of the outside of the piston, and then you have a punch in the shape of the inside. You just push it down and aluminum flows up in between the punch and outside die and forms in one push of three to five hundred tons pressure. You flow the aluminum when it's still pretty solid. It just flows like toothpaste into the form of the piston. And it's much stronger formed in that way than when you cast.

■   ■   ■

We have three "Dynos," which are all electronically controlled for speed. The first fundamental thing about the Dynamometer is you run the Indy engine at a set speed between 6,000 and 10,000 rpm, and you measure the actual horsepower being developed by the engine on that day. You optimize your emission setting to get your maximum power and set that on the Dynamometer, and you also decide how much fuel is the optimum setting for that engine, the injection setting. Therefore, we're able to get the power of that particular engine on that particular day. You then try them with correction factors so that if you tested the engine the following week, you would end up with the same power despite the fact that the weather conditions have changed. Unfortunately, the correction factors don't always correct adequately, and it is exceedingly difficult to carry out meaningful development of small things that are likely to give you small gains. There are tendencies in most people to do quick tests on engines and say, "Whoopee! I've made my engine twenty horsepower better than last week!" Most of this is an absolute myth, and most people who run Dynamometers don't run them hard enough or long enough to actually get any meaningful figures. But we get an accurate test in probably only seven or eight minutes, because we have done an hour's running in and settling and so on before doing that. But we also check things like the oil consumption of the engine and the blow-by past the pistons because that affects the oil scavengering. We have checks on the fuel injector, the amount of wear by leakage from mechanical fuel pumps, metering units, a whole collection of things. We obviously check our oil flow. Quite often we check the temperature rise in the oil through the engine and see if the water temperature is meaningful and correct. We have about six monometers that control different pressures around the engines, and by taking readings, we can judge their general condition and whether they're likely to survive the next race.

Opposite and above right: A Cosworth worker uses tongs to remove a newly born piston from the die assembly of the forge. It is crated with hundreds of others (*top right*), and sent through a series of precise machining, boring, and inspection stages. *Bottom right:* A finished set of eight awaits assembly to the block. *Overleaf:* The completed (2600cc) turbocharged V-8 engine about to be run up to full power and tested on one of Cosworth's three Dynamometers.

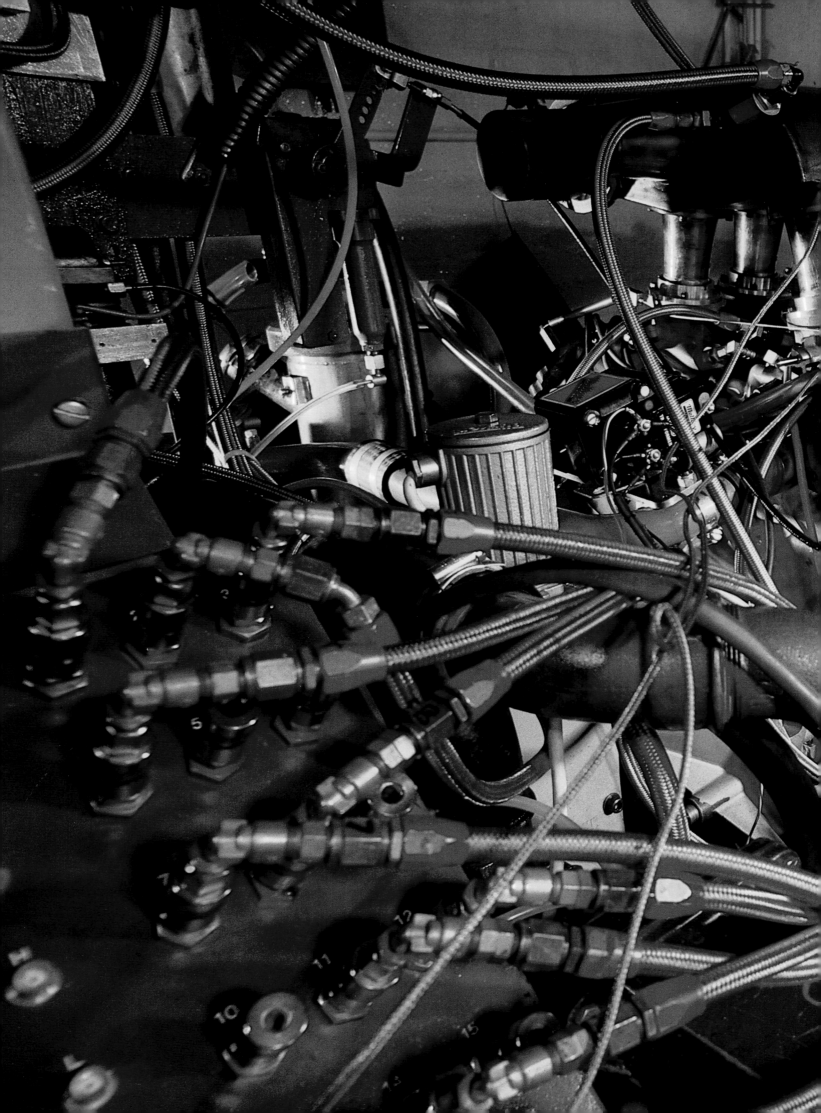

Keith Duckworth:

We decided that we could only sell the engine in a basic form. You obviously can't make an exhaust system to suit every car, therefore you haven't got an exhaust system. We do make a recommendation of what the parts should look like. We test the engine on the test bed here with a slave exhaust system and turbocharger and our slave plenum chamber, and we set up the fuel injection system for each individual engine as well. It's obviously complete with all its water and oil pumps, and we have recommendations for oil tank design and the plumbing arrangement. Our plumbing stops with what is essential to connect parts in the engine and doesn't include the plumbing that connects the engine to the car's oil tank. So it is a tested engine apart from plenum chamber, exhaust system, and turbocharger.

Tony Cicale:

I think what your eye sees are the details, and you see a more pleasing shape only because it has a nicer radius or nicer blends, or it doesn't have these sharp edges where the body comes together. That's nothing you ever really design into a car, but it's always a plus if the car looks nice after it's done. Quite honestly, there are certain areas that don't seem to be particularly important in the performance of the car. When you sit down to draw them, you try to sculpt them so they're pleasing aesthetically, but it's not a styling exercise per se.

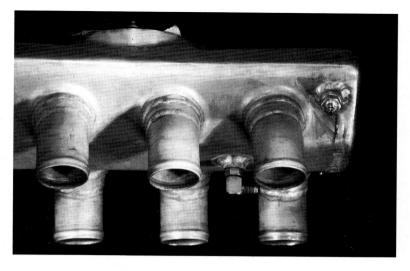

An intake log, or manifold (*above*), similar to one in place atop engine block in rear view (*opposite*). The tubular extensions connect directly to the tops of the cylinder head assemblies.

Bobby Unser, Driver:

If I thought I had something good going, a concept with the car or a new direction—it might be something we thought it needed—but it still was a gamble. So Dan Gurney would say, "Can't have it." It would be that simple. There would be a lot of arguments, usually months of it. And then you lost, because you can't scream with Dan. You can't say, "Give it to me or else." Dan always thought of himself as being the designer. Which was bad. He had a lot of good ideas, but his ideas didn't always fall in line with being practical. If Dan decided it's a no, it's a no. So, I'd tell my chief, Wayne Leary, "Hey, Gurney is not gonna let us try it. You got to get 'em made yourself." Well, Wayne's a fabricator. Besides being a good chief mechanic, the son of a bitch can fabricate parts. He can bend and weld metal. Doesn't need a designer. So I said, "Wayne, we got to have her. I know you're busy, but make it." That guy can make magic. He'd do it at night when Gurney doesn't even know what's going on. Now this didn't happen often, but it happened on occasion. I always got my stuff. It just was harder to get. If you couldn't get in the front door, you went around to the back.

Jackie Howerton:

The problem is not to make it. It's to make it fit. If you just made a motor cover that didn't have to fit anything, you could build it real fast. The problem is that the car's got all kinds of little odd shapes and angles. It has to miss the turbocharger and intake manifold and still lay flat on the back of the tub. Your first thought is, "Damn, how do I get that to go everywhere it's supposed to go? How do I know where it's supposed to go?" Well, you don't, so you have to research the thing, sit down and make some little drawings and templates. If you're good enough to make that stuff, you develop all kinds of little trick methods of measuring things and holding things and making little templates and fixtures, and the next thing you know, you've done it. And actually building it doesn't take that much time. The time is in figuring out how to build it and in making sure in engineering the thing that it fits. When you look at that piece that's the part you don't see.

A typical Indy car turbocharger consists of a compressor and a turbine connected by a common shaft.

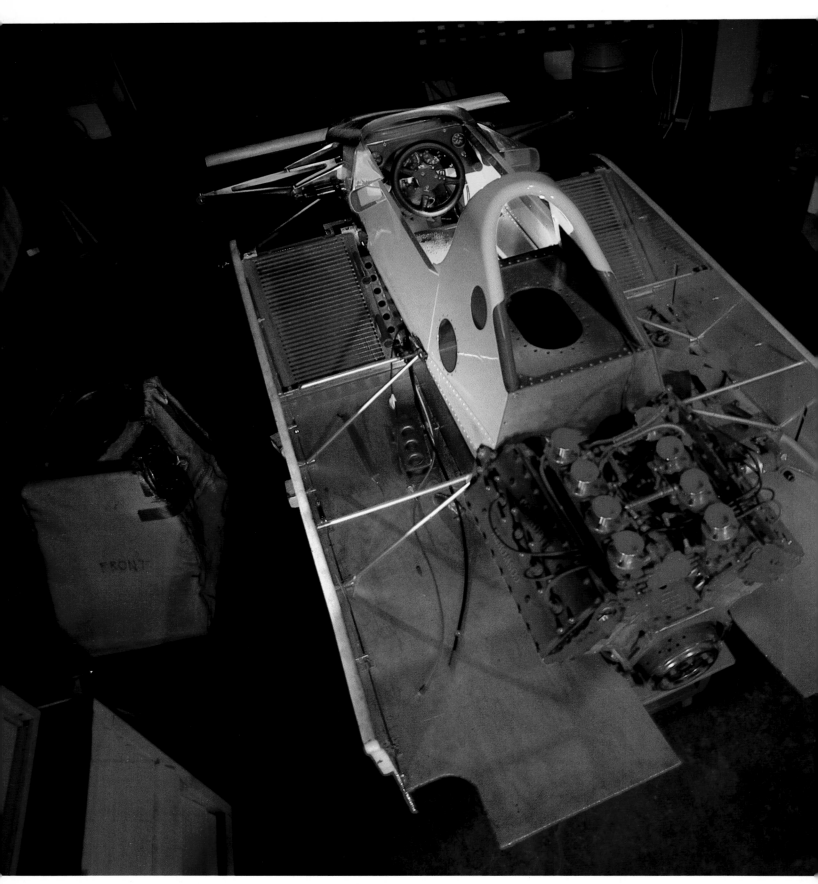

Above: With the motor in place behind the tub, the sidepod components and radiators are next to be attached. The underbody of each pod, made from large sheets of honeycombed aluminum, is carefully shaped to match the aerodynamic contours determined from the wind-tunnel test. The car's crash-worthy nylon fuel cell sits on the shop floor (*at left*) awaiting installation in the tub immediately in front of the motor.

THE TUB BECOMES A RACE CAR

Robin Herd:

To my mind, the job of the designer is not to have all the bright ideas, but to get together all the bright ideas, pick the best of them, and use them. They may very often come from the fabricators.

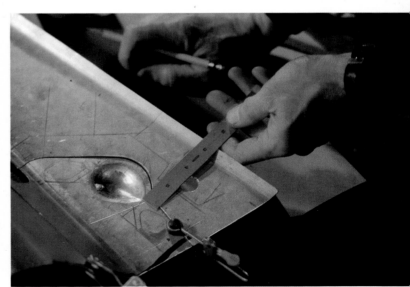

George Heuning:

A lot of parts are built without a drawing. Here are all the surrounding parts; now connect this to that, with this in mind.

67

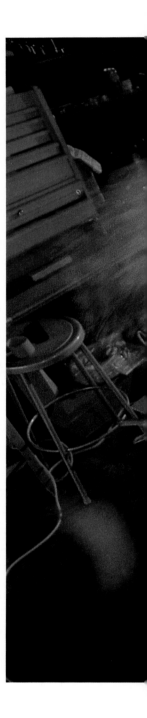

Tracey Potter, Mechanic:

You do a lot of little "knickknack stuff," like pedals, brackets that hold things, and radiator mounts. It's all the little stuff that takes forever to do, and at first it seems really confusing until you really dig in and get after it.

Michael Wolther, Mechanic:

You get close as a team when you're actually building the car together and working to a common goal. You can see all this labor and I guess love, too, that we put into this thing, and finally it was real. We'd actually made this car, and it had all the potential in the world. We didn't know then that it was a sled. We thought it was the most beautiful thing. It was the only car we'd ever built, so we were proud of it. It may not be a real piece of art when viewed as a whole, but there was some really beautiful components on it. Even the guys who do the real thankless jobs felt then like they were making something pretty neat. Actually doing it with our hands. That was a good feeling. It made me feel real close to the guys I was working with, and I don't think we've ever really been that close since.

George Heuning:

Your mind starts to falter, you're tired, and your body gets burned out. But you have to do it, so you do it. When you think of something that has to be done, you can't put it off for a minute, because you'll probably forget about it. Finishing a new race car under pressure is like getting a sore tooth pulled after you've struggled through a three-day holiday with this tremendous ache in your mouth. Everybody knows how that feels. Goddamn, we did it! Everybody kind of looks around and pats each other on the back when that thing is going out the door and getting loaded on the truck. At that point you're so tired and worn out you're not really thinking about how well it's going to do. Of course that's in the back of your mind, but the biggest feeling is just relief.

George Heuning:

All fabricators have some artist in them, because they must have a good eye and be able to interpret what they see on the drawing. People are always expecting them to work miracles. The designer sits down and makes a twenty-minute drawing and sends it to us figuring it takes twenty minutes to build the part. But that doesn't happen.

Michael Wolther:

We couldn't have built a second car if we'd crashed that thing in testing or practice. To get the thing ready, we had been coming in at eight o'clock in the morning and going home at ten every night, seven days a week. We forgot what our families looked like. You couldn't even think of taking the day off. It was just like, "Why don't I fly to the moon?"

THE CAR'S FIRST TEST

Bobby Unser:

The guy that designs a new race car always thinks that it's the best that there ever was. The guy that fabricated the car has to think the same thing. So the guy that finances it is naturally going to think the same thing. It's gonna be the finest that ever was born. But it isn't gonna be. Usually it's gonna be a shit box to start with. Unfortunately that's just a fact of life. Once in a blue moon a car is very quick, what we call "off the trailer," but very seldom. So as a test driver, you have to realize that the first time you get in it, it's going to have some faults. Your job is to try to find out what those faults are. Is it a suspension problem? Is it an air problem? Is it just a track savvy problem? — meaning the adjustments like camber, cross weight springs, sway bars, and things like that. Understand you've got people who want views on it quickly, but you can't really do that. So you've got to put all these people off. You got to keep your own head straight. My system is not to see how fast you can go in it, because that's the most deceiving thing in the world. In other words, don't qualify the car when you're testing it. Test the car. You have to keep telling yourself this, because a lot of drivers feel that speed is the only thing that counts. But if you test going too fast, you're just sitting there saving your life all the time. You're running so hard you're just trying to keep from crashing, and you're not feeling anything the car is telling you. But you can't do this real slow either. Why more guys can't test I don't know. I sit back and I laugh about it, because so many race car drivers are nonmechanical people. Testing really has to do with being able to go the proper speed to let the race car tell you what it wants to tell you. Sometimes you don't know how to talk to it or listen to it, but it will tell you what the problems are. When it's feeling bad, the most important thing to realize is that maybe you're a good driver. It's too easy for a guy to say, "Well, it's really not the car, it's a mistake I'm making. I'm not up today." Well, that's bullshit. First of all, you have to believe in yourself. Never doubt yourself, because every time you do, the old race car will get away from you. You must have the utmost confidence in yourself. So how long does it take? If you started in November, you could get the car working pretty good by the Indianapolis race in May.

Al Unser, Sr.:

You don't know what a brand new race car is going to do, or how it's going to perform, so a driver has to be very careful when he first goes out with it. Try the brakes, the steering, and make sure when you stand on it going down the straightaway, it goes straight. When you back off the throttle very abruptly, does it want to dive to the left or the right? You slowly work up the speed over a few laps. Then you have to start extending yourself and taking some chances. I just put it into the corners faster and faster, and try to find where the car doesn't like to be and where it likes to be. You search it out. But you never know when it's gonna bite you. Running at such a fine line, when it does bite back or jumps loose, you can't always say, "Well, I know what happened." Once you hit that wall, it's so damn tore up, you don't know whether something broke, whether you made the mistake or the car made the mistake. So when you test a new car, it really gets on a guy's nerves.

George Heuning:

Anybody with any sense is not going to thrash the car right away. He just goes out and warms up, takes a few laps, maybe four or five at less than one hundred miles an hour, and comes back in. You tell him to get out of the car you jack it up, and you look at this and wiggle that and shake this and kick that and try to see if anything's falling off. If he's got any comments about the thing doing anything strange, you want to hear them.

Carl Haas, Owner:

You can't just look at it and say it's a great race car, you have to be intimately involved in it to know about it. It's an evolutionary thing. Take the Lola T-800 for example. I was involved with it for over a year. We knew going in, from the wind tunnel research and detail in chassis construction and stiffness, that it would be a good race car. Things are subtle and very sophisticated. You just can't eyeball it and see the advantages.

INDY CAR SPECIFICATIONS

ENGINE:	*2.65 litre Cosworth DFX Turbocharged V-8*
TRANSMISSION:	*Hewland DGB Transaxle (4-speed, ovals; 5-speed, road)*
GEARING:	*(4-speed Indy)* *1st: 9.55* *2nd: 6.09* *3rd: 4.15* *4th: 4.10*
COOLING SYSTEM:	*Sidepod mounted brass fin and tube radiators*
STEERING:	*Rack and pinion (1.75 turns to lock)*
WHEELS:	*Cast magnesium alloy, single nut fixing* *Front: 15 x 10 inches.* *Rear: 15 x 14 inches*
FUEL SYSTEM:	*Single central Goodyear safety fuel cell; 40 gallon capacity*
FUEL:	*Methanol*
CHASSIS:	*High-sided carbon fiber and aluminum honeycomb monocoque. Engine is fully stressed unit and rear suspension is mounted off transmission casing and bellhousing*
BRAKES:	*Outboard mounted A. P. hydraulic four-piston calipers acting on ventilated discs (Driver adjusted brake bias)*
BODY:	*Carbon fiber, kevlar, and honeycomb composites. Venturi sidepods. Front and rear adjustable carbon fiber wings*
FRONT SUSPENSION:	*Fabricated upper and lower wishbones. Top wishbones actuate inboard dampers and coil springs mounted outboard of Venturi. Cast magnesium alloy uprights*
REAR SUSPENSION:	*Fabricated upper and lower wishbones and lower track control rod. Dampers and coil springs mounted outboard of Venturi. Cast magnesium alloy uprights*
DIMENSIONS:	*Length: 180 inches; Width: 78.5 inches; Wheelbase: 109 inches; Weight: 1,550 pounds*

George Heuning:

You want to go out and get the car shook down, and you're just kind of praying to yourself that you haven't overlooked anything. The prime concern in my mind at all times is that there's a human being sitting in that thing. I've had the unfortunate experience to be on two different teams that have lost drivers, and I spent a lot of sleepless nights because of it, wondering if it was possibly something I left loose or did wrong to cause this guy to lose his life. I laid in bed at night and cried, wondering if it was something I did.

Al Unser, Sr., takes his new car out for the first time.

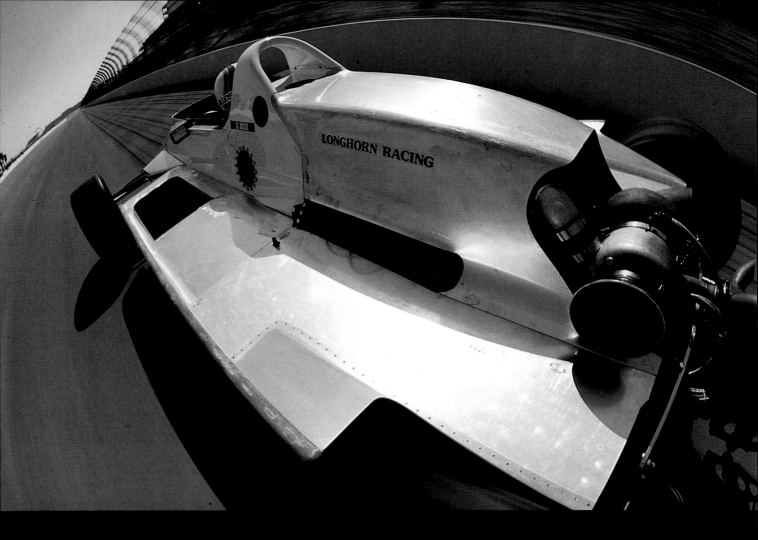

Mario Andretti:

Let's face it, when you first get with "the beast," you still don't have the confidence of it. You've got to get away with a couple of pretty close calls, and feel, "Man, this baby is saving my ass!"

PART **2**

RITUALS

Richard Fried:

Sometimes, we've been up since six o'clock that morning. We have to load the truck, work all day long, and then do a thirteen-hour drive. We usually get there about six the next morning. People don't realize that.

Phil Casey, Crew Chief:

From tire testing you keep track of your changes and spring rates and everything, and then you set up the car in the shop before you leave. You also have your setups from the times you ran races there before.

Wally Dallenbach, Driver:

It's very difficult to get the job done, even with the best equipment, because there's fierce competition. The people who make them run are very special people, and they all share the same feeling of commitment. Of course there's a lot of sacrifice that goes along with it. It's very demanding. You're on the road a lot of hours, and you're often faced with disappointment. That all comes with the package.

GETTING THERE

George Heuning:

Unpacking is no problem. Just like opening your suitcase and dumping everything out. It's getting it all back in that's the problem. That's a hassle. Usually you're unpacking under better conditions than you're packing. No crowds and plenty of time.

Phil Casey:

When you go to places like Pocono, there's not much equipment or anything there. So the transporter carries a small drill press, a lathe, a heliarc welding unit, all that stuff. When you get there, if you break something you won't have any problem trying to find the right equipment to fix it. You have everything there to work with. We even bring materials to fabricate anything we want.

Richard Fried:

When you first get there, the biggest priority is to get the car out and the heaters plugged in for the oil. Then set up any trackside "spares" on the golf cart and get the tool boxes out. From that point on, just unload whatever equipment you need for working on the car in the garage. You slowly build up all your pit stuff—nitrogen bottles, timing stand, and fuel tank—and move it out to the line. We have a certain number of boxes that hold various maintenance pieces: spare nuts and bolts and tie wraps. We usually keep them on the golf cart. We get the wheels out right away and take them over to the Goodyear tent or garage. Then they mount the tires for you.

Overleaf: Indy cars under preparation are viewed from a ceiling camera high over the floor of the Long Beach Arena.

LOOKING AFTER DETAILS

Howard Gilbert, Engine Builder:

We prefer to burn the midnight oil before we get there. We have a feeling that the minute you unload, you should be ready. Of course you break things, and you come into situations that are unforeseen. But if you're well prepared before you get to the racetrack, you have extra equipment and you've foreseen a lot of possibilities. Those all-nighters can be very frustrating, because you get dull in your thinking. That's why we bring extra engines and extra cars.

Richard Fried:

Since you're all cooped up in the garage, or you're on the road and don't get to see that many people outside, racers wind up being your only acquaintances. It's a friendly battle you have against these guys all the time, because you see them more than you see anybody else.

Hywel Absalom, Crew Chief:

I consider myself to be a professional person who's getting paid to do a job, and my worth is only as great as what I produce. The biggest problem with the job is controlling the people who work for me as well as the people I work for, like the driver.

Phil Casey:

You tend to become good friends with the other people involved in racing, because you're all so close together. You do all these things together. If you need something, you borrow it from somebody. If you're in a bind at a racetrack and you have a problem, they bring you things, and it works both ways.

A. J. Watson, Crew Chief:

Good young mechanics are hard to find. Most kids you hire today want to be the chiefs right off...like working on engines instead of just doing "stooge's work." They'd rather do things they can't do.

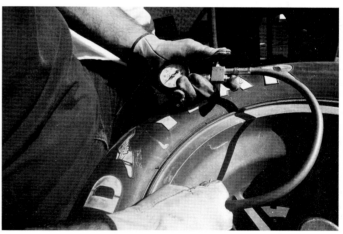

Opposite, above: A. J. Foyt (*right*) and his long-time engine builder, Howard Gilbert, warm up their Cosworth engine while observing the autograph seekers outside the Pocono garages. *Opposite, below:* Crew chief Tyler Alexander checks the plug wiring after a warm-up period at Indianapolis.

THE TIME GETS NEAR

Carl Haas:

As it gets more competitive, more and more technology creeps into it. You need specialists with expertise in engineering, good mechanics, a good crew chief, a good team manager, and good engine people. You could have a great race car and a poor driver, and it won't get it done, or a great driver and a poor car and you'll get the same result. You must have the whole package if you're going to be winning with any kind of consistency.

Al Unser, Sr.

A. J. Foyt.

Al Unser, Sr.:

I think about it twenty-four hours a day. I don't have a problem with getting myself ready, I'm ready at all times. What bothers me is when I get there and my car's not finished or my crew's confused. That disturbs me. Nothing makes me happier than getting to the racetrack, walking in the garage, and seeing my car and crew ready. It gets me keyed up and I say to myself, "Well, now it's my turn."

As the time for practice approaches, cars are towed out to the pit area.

Mario Andretti:

The moment I put on my uniform and my gear all of a sudden I go into a kind of trance. I walk away from this life and step into another, and I find that I cannot fully relax when I have it on....I feel like I am "on duty." You've got that on. It's for a purpose. You're doing a job.

Rick Mears:

A lot of people feel that speed is what everybody in racing is after; we're all speed demons, that's what we enjoy. For me the speed doesn't really have anything to do with it, as long as I'm the first one there. That's the part that gets my attention. It's the competition.

Bill Vukovich, Driver:

I don't think you have to get yourself up. I think it's just natural. If a guy has to work at it, he doesn't belong in a race car. You don't have to work on getting mean. It comes. The closer you get to the deadline, the guys get mean.

Below: Mario Andretti (*right*) makes a point to car owner Carl Haas (*kneeling*) and Tony Cicale (*center*).

Below: Bobby Unser. *Opposite:* Crew chief George Bignotti briefs Kevin Cogan.

Hywel Absalom:

If you're quick, you're quick, and you'd be quick any time of the day. Some people think it's the wind and the weather. I don't.

Jim Hall:

If you've got the car capable of running fast and everybody knows it, I think it probably makes a lot of sense to just go out there and run fast from the beginning.

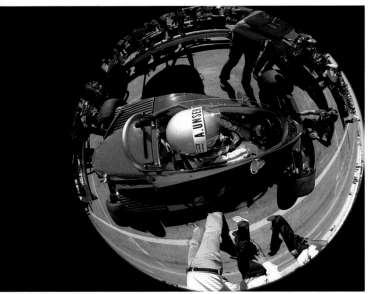

Al Unser, Sr.:

We wear so much stuff around our bodies the public doesn't recognize us when we get out of the car. They don't relate to us as real people. They say, "You really race cars, you're Al Unser? Well, you don't look like him." Hell, I've always got a helmet on. How could I?

Above: Mario Andretti (*far left*) and members of the Newman/Haas Racing crew wait out the final minutes before practice begins.

Dan Gurney, Team Manager:

It's not a good spot for someone who has problems with claustrophobia. It's really important that it does fit you like a glove, because you depend on the car to support you going around the corners. If you find that you're having to hold the steering wheel just to keep you upright, then you can't drive fast. You've got to be able to lean on this car, and it's got to fit you all the way around.

Mike Mosley, Driver:

It's kind of a security blanket. You're in there all snug and nice and tight. You got a helmet on your head, and you're kind of like in a cave. You can't see if there's a guy up on your right rear, because your mirrors are mostly between the engine and the wheels, mostly straight back. Your peripheral vision is only so far.

Overleaf: Mario Andretti in the cockpit of his Lola.

93

Above: Crew chief John Capels discusses a handling problem with Bill Vukovich.
Below: Geoff Brabham climbs into the cockpit of his March Indy car.
Opposite: Danny Ongais, already belted in, awaits the green light.

Mario Andretti:

The competitor in Formula One is faceless. In the event of an accident or something, I am very cold about those things and I couldn't care less. It's just another one out of the way. Awful, awful way to think, but I just don't have that feeling for them…they're too distant. Here at home, I can get to know the guys more intimately to a degree that I'm not sure which one I like best at different times.

Wally Dallenbach:

We drivers have a unique relationship. We understand each other's problems, but we're not close. You can be friends and buddies, but your job is to beat them. It's tough to be chummy and yet beat the guy out of his money. So you have this understanding. It's very common to share handling problems, which is probably the single biggest thing one driver talks to another driver about. If you're going faster than your buddies, they want to know why. It's the game of speed.

GREEN LIGHT

Mario Andretti:

I like to be the first one out. I think this is a big game of psych, just to let everybody know you're ready and that your machine is ready. Somebody else could be still screwing around the garage. That's good. I like to get the jump on everybody as fast as I can, even when conditions are not as clean.

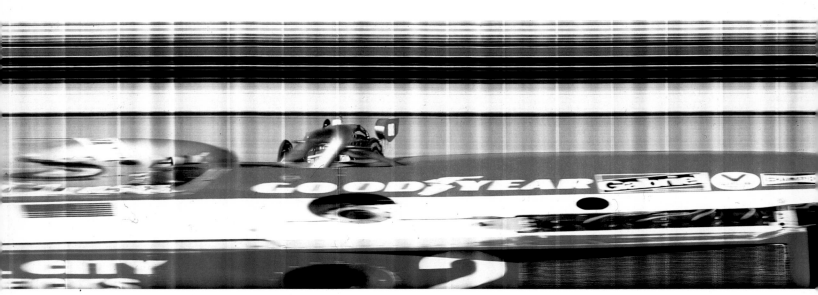

George Heuning:

The conditions from the opening practice session until it comes time to qualify are worlds apart, and I think a lot of people start jacking around with their chassis settings too soon. They go out there and the racing surface is dirty, it doesn't have any rubber on it. So when the track finally gets into shape, they're out in left field somewhere. We let the track tune to us rather than us tune to the track.

Denis Daviss, Chief Mechanic:

Normally we like to let somebody else go out first. Once the dust is gone, then what you do is what you do. When it's still dusty, the thing is a bit "squirrely," and you might think something's wrong with the car. It's just picking up the dust, running on the "marbles," as we call it. You can't drive quick on a load of marbles. So we like to let other people run first, and blow the shit off.

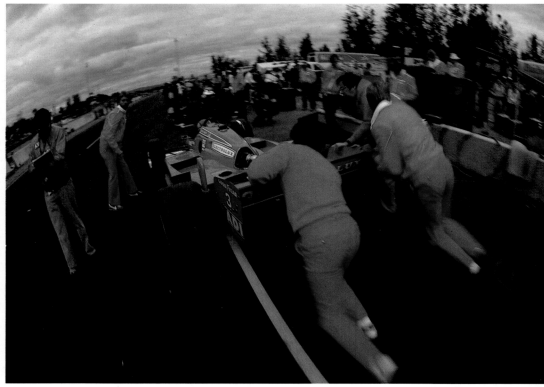

Michael Andretti runs through "turn one" at Indianapolis.

Michael Andretti, Driver:

A lot of noise, a lot of vibration. If you're behind somebody, your head really starts moving around. You just feel wind forcing you around and it's very uncomfortable.

Bobby Rahal, Driver:

There's a beauty to oval track racing in that it's like the difference between a civilian helicopter and a "Cobra" gunship. One is built to do many things, the other is built for one thing. I think that's what's so fascinating about Indy cars. There's a purity there that's kind of neat, but road racing for me is the most enjoyable form of racing. I think it's the more taxing form, both mentally and physically, because it's always a compromise. Oval track racing isn't. To be successful, there can be no compromise, and I think that's what makes it so appealing.

A driver's-eye view, heading down the front straight at Indianapolis.

Rick Mears:

You stay on the throttle as you enter the corner, and start dropping down. If you're working really well, you can keep on it all the way down the middle, where the G forces really start picking up. You're feeling the side load down low, and you have to roll out of the throttle just as you get close to the center of the corner. If you don't, the power will override the car, and it'll start climbing the bank. You've got to get off the throttle there, just enough to let the car settle, and let the suspension come into effect. That keeps the nose planted so it will stay on the bottom of the track. As you go through the middle of the turn you're just about flat back on the throttle.

GETTING UP TO SPEED

Gordon Johncock, Driver:

As you're coming around the corner, you're not really watching the wall, you're watching for the other guy. If you're looking at the wall, and he makes a little move and you're not paying attention, it might just be too late to get away from him.

HOT LAPS

Michael Andretti:

When you first get in, everything is new to you again. You come in after the first few laps and see that you were three seconds off the pace, and you think, "There's no way, I must have lost it, something's not right." But after you run a few more laps, you get right into the rhythm of things. You have to get your eyes looking at the right points, because your eye contact is very important. I think at Indy it takes a while to get used to the speeds, and you're not looking far enough ahead. You look at an object and you're there already; you need to look way ahead. In road racing you get to the corner and you're looking at the apex, and once you clip the apex, you're looking at the outside. On a high-speed oval, you have to be looking to the outside and as far ahead as you can see, because there's not much time.

Above: The long climb up the hill to "turn four" at Elkhart Lake, a beautiful road course.

Tom Sneva, Driver:

Sometimes when a car isn't working right, all of a sudden you start thinking you're not sitting right and there isn't enough padding here, or too much there, and the steering wheel is not quite right. You start thinking about things that maybe are causing you not to go as quickly as you feel you should be. But usually it's not the cockpit comfort. It's because the chassis itself doesn't feel very good. It's amazing that a twenty-five-pound spring change in just one corner will make such a big difference. Before the thing was a complete stranger to you.

Rick Mears:

The first time out, you've got to acclimate yourself to the car and to the speed. It always takes a couple of laps to do that. After running a while, everything's clockwork, and it feels slow. You're driving into the corner, and you've got plenty of time to think. That's cause you're acclimated to the car and the speed you're running. Then you get out of the car for a week. When you get back in and you go down to that same corner and try to shut off at the same point, goddamn! It feels like you're in that corner so quick and deep and everything is happening too fast. Everything's a blur. You come back in. They say, "Okay, what was the oil temperature? How many rpms?" Well, bullshit! "Are you kidding me? Take my eyes off the road long enough to look at those things? You're crazy." You've got to run a few laps and get dialed into it again. Then you start looking at the tach coming off every corner. You look at the oil pressure every straightaway. Cause you're more acclimated to the speed and you've got time to think.

Above: Streaking over the start/finish line beneath the starter's platform at Michigan International Speedway.

Rick Mears:

The fans know we're running two hundred miles an hour, but they don't know what that means. They have no idea. I usually put it that we're covering a football field in a second. And that kind of gives them an idea, because they know what a football field looks like. When they're up in the stands watching from a distance, the cars don't look like they're really running that fast. Another thing is the reason people like stock cars so much; they can run close. Fans don't realize it, but we can't run close. That's when we get in trouble, cause our cars depend on the air for downforce. When we get close to somebody the wings "go away." The cars won't handle.

116

John Barnard:

If it's right you have enormous rushing of air and so on, but there shouldn't be a lot of buffeting for the driver. It's a fairly smooth ride.

Below: Bobby Rahal rides through "turn four" of Milwaukee's historic one-mile oval.

Denis Daviss:

The watch rules our existence. We get up in the morning, have breakfast, and go to the track to a watch. Then we go around and around all day to another watch. In racing, it's *the* element. It doesn't matter if the driver says, "Yeah, it feels real good." If the watch says it's not quick enough, then the watch takes precedence. And you say, "You're only going this quick. It oughta feel good at that speed."

Bobby Rahal:

The tighter you are in the car the better, obviously within reason. With the forces that you're going through, there can be no extra room. You have to be comfortable, but very tight, so you can feel what the car is saying. If you're "hanging on" all the time, flopping around in there, you aren't going to get the proper feedback.

CONFERENCE TIME

Rick Mears:

There are race car drivers, and then there are race car drivers. Some of them drive race cars, and others, the race cars drive them. You've got to be able to explain in words that others can understand exactly what the car is doing. There's no coming in and saying, "Well, I don't know."

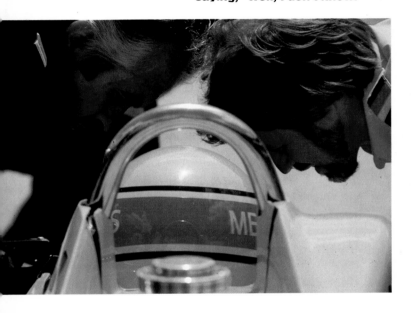

Bobby Unser:

It's being right in what you say and what you decide. Because when the driver comes in and he tells the designer this is the way it is, that's got to be gospel. Otherwise the poor designer goes off into his own closet and starts in the wrong direction. This is where most teams get hurt. A driver is better off saying, "I don't understand," and letting it lay. Don't just reach in your hip pocket, pull out an idea, and say, "This is what I think it is." Then everything that follows is going to be worse.

George Bignotti, Crew Chief:

You get to be a good guesser. A lot of times the driver will come in and say it's doing something, and he's not expressing himself just right. Checking the tire temperatures will tell you what it's really doing...whether the front end is pushing or whether it's loose. You have to pay attention, because he's driving it, but you always make sure that what he's telling you is right.

Steve Roby, Crew Chief:

I don't believe in drivers being engineers. Depends on the driver, of course, but I haven't met one yet that's been any good. The driver you want is the driver who comes in and says, "The car is doing this." Period.

Mario Andretti confers with Tony Cicale before returning to the track.

Bill Simpson, Driver:

A good chief mechanic is not only a mechanic, he's a psychologist. He doesn't realize it, but he is. He asks questions of you, and the way he asks that question can get two answers 180 degrees apart. He has to understand who his driver is and where he's at.

Tom Sneva:

A race car will only do two things: either it will "push," or it will be "loose." If it is "pushing," when you go to the corner and start to turn, it will want to go straight ahead. "Loose" is when you're going to turn in, the front end is very positive, and that will want to kick the rear end around.

Tony Cicale:

I've driven before, and I understand how important, how much of this game is really mental—and how much of it is a question of confidence. Everyone on the team has to have confidence in their abilities, and once they lose that, it becomes a difficult, frightful situation because of the pressures and the dangers. The driver in particular. Part of my job is to try to help him maintain his confidence. It's absolutely essential he feels he has someone he can rely on for accurate, honest information. And if something is going wrong with the car, you try to reassure him that things will be worked out and changes will be made to his liking. Even great ones like Mario at times question their confidence and abilities. So there always has to be someone he can really depend on, not to give him a massage job or tell him, "Mario, you're fantastic." But to sit him down and say, "Look, calm down. Things aren't going so great right now, but we'll sort them out." Without being a driver, I wouldn't recognize how important the driver's frame of mind is to lap times once he sits in that car.

Leo Mehl, Goodyear Racing Chief:

"Stagger," by definition, is a differential in diameter between a left tire and a right tire. When you're racing on an oval and turning left, our engineers run a stagger depending on the driver's personal preference or his chassis's characteristics. For example, a one-tenth-of-an-inch stagger means that the right tire is one-tenth of an inch larger in diameter than the left tire. You often see them measuring with the "diameter tapes" to determine if the right tire is still at one-tenth of an inch. You've got the problem where you normally run more pressure in the right rear than you do in the left rear, so the right side gets hotter than the left.

Overleaf: Mario Andretti chases his son Michael (*at right*) and Geoff Brabham through the first turn at Indianapolis.

Tyler Alexander, Team Manager:
It's hot, sweaty, dirty, and a pain in the ass!

George Heuning:

Anything you have to do when you're at a racetrack involves bending over. By the end of the day, your back is just about ready to break in half. Sometimes you wish you had just a garage. One time it started raining and Gordy got off the course and tore a nose off the car. So we were drilling and standing out in the rain trying to work on the race car. We had electric drills and we were all afraid we were going to get electrocuted.

Richard Fried:

Some changes are pretty easy, and others are hard. It's a matter of designing the car to be changed quickly. Like the setup we have on our wing. Just take a couple of bolts out and slide the wing down and put the bolts back in, wind 'em up, and go. Changing springs you have to take the shock off, and that gets to be a big act. Of course, if you know what you want to do ahead of time you can have other shocks and springs already set up.

Rick Mears:

Naturally, the quickest way to run these cars is loose, but that's also the most dangerous way. You can run loose for a while, but eventually it will bite you. You learn to work from a feeling you get just before the car gets loose instead of waiting until the car gets loose to feel it. The rear end starts coming around just before the tires actually break adhesion. Most any other type of driving I've ever been in, at the slower speeds you can actually get in hot enough, let the car slide, and then catch it. In these cars, by the time it starts to slide, you better have already been catching it, or it's gone. You have to work off that feeling you get. It's a very fine feeling, hard to learn, and it's never for sure. There's something telling you, "It's gonna go loose, it's gonna go loose." The thing you've got to remember is that your ass doesn't lie to you. You've just got to pay attention to it.

Mario Andretti:

I always look at driving in the wet as a sequence of changing conditions— "wet" is wet, but it can be "wetter" and "rivers." The first problem is visibility. I mean, it's not only the fact that your car is ready to go out from under you at any moment, it's the surprise when you're following somebody with a big cloud in front of you, and you can't see the big puddle you're going to be crossing. Then you're gonna aquaplane. Sometimes it's just a wall of spray in front of you, and the only visibility you have is by looking out to the side—the only direction you can see. You just hope to remember where you are and where you're gonna turn. Wet conditions have produced some of the most anxious moments I've ever experienced. I parallel it with dirt-track driving, because there you get blasted so hard with the dirt you just can't see no matter how many cover lenses you have. So you have the advantage when you're up in front. At least you have the other guy in a cloud of mist, and you're raising hell with his visor.

Michael Andretti:

In a lot of ways it's totally opposite from driving in the dry. You try to stay away from the groove usually, and you actually look for dirt on the racetrack to get adhesion. You drive slow to go fast in the wet, brake early, and remember to get on the power slow and easy. You can't get too aggressive. That's when you can overdo it and spin. It's very easy to spin or to lock your brakes and overshoot the corners. So you have to be real calm.

Specially grooved tires hug the road as Michael Andretti approaches "turn five" in the rain at the Meadowlands road circuit.

Mario Andretti:

Besides the discomfort that everyone experiences, you prepare your helmet very differently. I try to come up with any concoction possible to put on my face shield to keep it from steaming. I've even had a personal friend who is a dentist go to a convention and try to come up with some kind of anti-fogging solution like they have for the mirrors they put in your mouth. The added problem we have, however, is changing temperatures, so it never worked well.

RUNNING IN THE WET

Al Unser, Sr.:

I've gone back out with a race car that's never been taken apart and dropped a ton of time. That's when you go back and you sit down and you look at the car and you say, "What the hell's different?" You start blaming each other. You're trying to find out from the mechanics what they changed. "Well, we never took it apart." "You didn't change engines?" "No, we didn't change engines." It's a very confusing time.

Bobby Rahal:

I think you start with the basics and then try to determine whether those things about that car can be changed in any way to further enhance it. Sometimes you'll do things that on paper look like they should work, but in reality they don't. And the opposite is also true, so it's a question of trial and error to a degree. But I think first you have to maximize what you have.

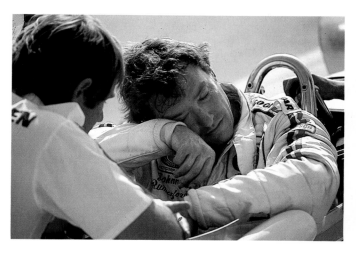

Tom Sneva:

You can be really frustrated when you've tried everything you can think of, and you get in that rut where nothing seems to help. You know you're not going through the corner as fast as somebody else, who has the same type of car you do, and that's pretty hard to take. There's nothing you can really do about an engine, so you just have to hope you can get the chassis working a little better.

Phil Casey:

Once in a while you get in a position where you start changing things and lose perspective. Say you lower the back of the car three turns and the front two. If you're making a lot of changes in a hurry, you can get the car pretty well out of balance without realizing it. Then you better go back and go through everything and regroup.

Above left: A crew chief signals the chief starter that his driver is about to begin his qualifying run.
Above right: Indianapolis safety patrolmen greet the new "pole sitter."

Mario Andretti prepares for what he hopes will be a record-breaking run for the pole at Indy.

Rick Mears:

Indy cars are so precise that if you can see the car do something with the naked eye, it's drastic. We're doing things constantly—sliding, turning, catching it—but it's all a minute deal. You can't see it with the naked eye, but we're feeling it. The wind's buffeting you around, but as you run and get comfortable, you get used to it. You kind of get your sea legs. You soon get to where you don't notice that things are moving. Everything seems to be fairly still. It's a little noisy, but you also get used to that. I try not to sense too many things, yet I try to sense everything. I don't want anything to distract me, but I've got to keep my mind open so in case something does change, I'll notice it. If the rpm sound changes a little bit, or the tone sound, you can tell if something's going wrong with the engine. You might get a little bit of a shake out of the car like something's coming loose. You've got to be aware at all times. Yet you can't let your mind go off. Concentration is the number one factor.

Mario Andretti:

Qualifying is a time when you don't even know your own name, and occasionally I go through it and forget a lot of things, because I'm like in a trance. You just don't want to be bothered with anything at all. The problem is that because you want to be alone, you look so accessible. You have so many people who think you need a word of encouragement, and you don't need anything. All you need is yourself at that point. The autograph seekers and the well-wishers are not welcome. That's the only time when I can become rude and the only time I don't feel guilty being rude, because I don't feel I need to explain my job to anyone. Those four laps you do in front of the world that first day of qualifying are when you are trying to do the best job you can ever come up with. And you want to be sure you squeeze that goddamn lemon right down to the last drop, without making a mistake. Everything is just spur of the moment reaction time, and some of the limits you reach qualifying you never reach at any other time. I know, and everyone doing it knows, where you have to reach and how far you have to reach, whether a run is the fastest you had ever done or not. I'll guarantee you at that point I don't feel I could get another ounce out of that car without crashing.

Michael Andretti:

You really want to go. You see the bands still on the track, it's like it takes three days for that last half hour to go by. When somebody's talking to you, you don't even recognize who it is, because you're starting to get into your own thinking pattern. You just want to really make sure you don't make a mistake and that you keep your head totally there. You pick out your points to look at, and you shoot for them. That's why eye contact is so important. If you look around you usually go where your eyes look. Sometimes when you're looking into the mirror you find yourself drifting out, so you try to always pick out your points time after time, lap after lap, and look at the same ones.

Wally Dallenbach:

The race is secondary, that's only five hundred miles and three and a half hours. You can be immortal a thousand times in that three and a half hours. In qualifying you only have a couple of minutes to be immortal. I find I'm much more apprehensive. At Indianapolis, it's the only time in a month you have the whole spotlight to yourself. For that reason it's important, and the superman comes out in everybody. When the chips are down, that last ounce of adrenaline comes out of you, and you just hang it out.

Overleaf: The garage area at Indianapolis, known as "Gasoline Alley," where mechanics prepare the qualified cars.

QUALIFYING

Howard Gilbert:

What concerns you is the rapidity with which you might have to do something very special, that really needs a little more time devoted to it. There's always that chance of slipping up and doing something wrong. That one little slip, when you don't have time to think about it and sort it out, can put an end to a year's work for a lot of people. This is the thing you think about most. You're checking for any flaws that might show up after you run them—cracks, breaks, chips—because pretty near every part in the race car is overstressed. If it's not overstressed, it's too heavy.

MAKING CHANGES

Bill Vukovich:

Well, they are getting paid to do a job, but it goes beyond that. They love racing. Or they wouldn't be doing it. They can probably make more money some other place. And I have never had a chief mechanic yet that I didn't appreciate. Because most of them, whether they are talented or not, they're doing the best job they can. They work their fingers right to the bone to try to get you in the race. A guy has got to appreciate that.

134

Scott Dennison, Mechanic:

It's not as comfortable as working in your own shop. You don't have the cars up on lifts, you have to crawl around on the floor. You're changing engines with a Mickey Mouse cherry picker rather than a nice overhead crane. It seems that the garages are usually either wet or cold or not lit properly. You never have enough electricity or enough room. You've got a lot of guys crowded into not much space, so it makes it a little bit more difficult to operate.

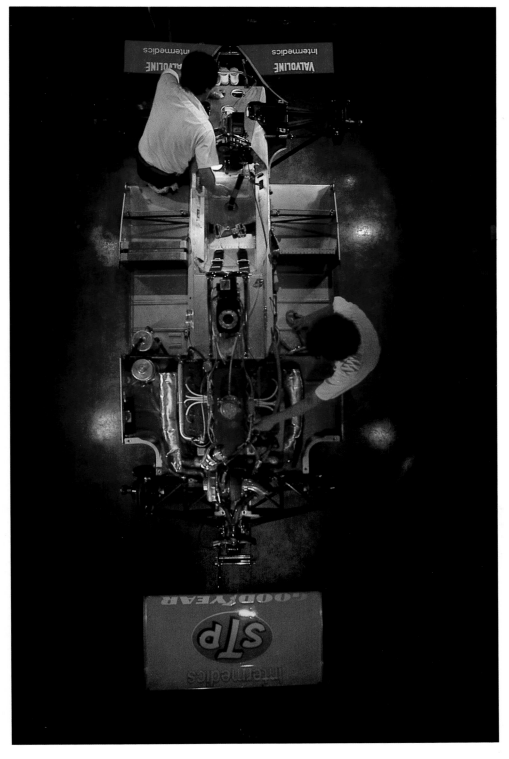

Eugene Grimm, Mechanic:

A lot of the work is repetition, so you really get familiar with what each pipe and line looks like. You've got dozens of them. But after you've done them a few times a year, you can recognize each one by the type of fittings on the end and the angles and all that. You just look at it and know it's a fuel line or an oil line. There's a great deal of difference in how a new engine is prepared. If you have to switch over all the components, it can turn into a six-hour job. If that's all prepared for you, it cuts it down to two hours, which can mean the difference between making or not making a race.

135

PART 3

THE CHASE

THE SHOW BEFORE THE RACE

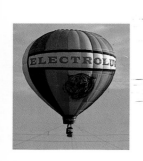

Above: The Electrolux Tiger holds court with Michael and Mario Andretti and Steve McMillan, president of Electrolux Corp.

Richard Fried:

At Indy, we get to the track at six o'clock A.M., and there's nobody in the stands. You turn around and go back out to the pit lane at ten, and there's jillions of people out there. You suddenly realize, "Jeez, look at the jillions of people!" There's just too much tension and the tension is going to get to your stomach after a while, so maybe you start smoking or chewing your fingernails. You just can't get too uptight. But Jesus Christ! Look at all these bands, look at all those people up in the stands! What are they doing here?

AM 9:46

Above: Mario Andretti, accompanied by his friend "Bud," sits in the driver's seat behind the Budweiser Clydesdales.

THOUGHTS TURN INWARD

Mario Andretti:

I don't like any wasteful talk because it makes your mind wander. I'll pop a joke sometimes just to get rid of the tension a little bit. But no small talk or any of that bullshit. I do like to hear the national anthem played because it is a touching moment and very appropriate. I find I get the same feeling inside—apprehension or anxiety. It's incredible. It is so important to win, and there is a feeling of, "What the hell am I going to have to do today to do it?" You just can't wait to be tossed in that ring to do the work. Those last five minutes are an eternity. Because all of a sudden you are counting the time. It is slow. Five minutes is forever. So many things go through your mind.

Bill Simpson:

We decide the night before what our strategy will be. There's a lot of discussion over the back of the wing before the race. "Oh, look at that blonde over there." It's sort of frivolous talk really. Not much substance. It always seems before any race, whether it's Indy or any of the other races, the mechanics all seem to walk around more nervous than I am. They can get pretty grumpy.

Dan Gurney:

All the old things are true. The atmosphere is so thick, you can darn near cut it with a knife. At Indy it's the culmination of a month's build-up, and there's a huge crowd there waiting. Time has a funny way of moving slow and digging you. Then it's accelerating. It's coming. There's a funny feeling of tick, tock, tick, tock. In a few hours the thing will be over. Everybody will know who won and why.

Tom Sneva:

Everybody knows the proper thing to do, but the adrenaline is flowing so hard that sometimes we do things that we wouldn't normally do because we are so pumped up. You have to really psych yourself down and make yourself think, okay, it's a long race. Don't worry about passing two or three guys early. Just stay out of trouble.

Bobby Rahal:

I like to be in the motor home with close friends and stay out of the noise and the dirt and the heat. I give myself some time to get my thoughts together, and for an hour or so before a race, I'll try to be totally alone. Just to think about what I'm about to do. That may take fifteen minutes or what have you, but once I'm done with that, I'm ready.

Dan Gurney:

It's a very special group. You know that within a short time, you're going to be out there in this hostile environment together. It's interesting to feel the others—how they're coping with that situation, either through the small talk or the smart aleck or the sense of humor. That's something special that only a driver can go through; and he can sense how the other guys are taking it.

Wally Dallenbach:

I constantly rehash my chances. How competitive will I be? Take a good look around. See how things are going. You utter a short prayer and wait. Don't try to take my thoughts away from me. I need them. So a joke I don't need. It's in bad taste. I feel the important thing is for me to think about the next hour or so—and me. After that I'm going to be pushed into action.

Denis Daviss:

You wish everyone a good race, which is fair. Unlike a lot of other things in this world, where people wish the other person harm, we wish him not to get it. Guy's going good and he's gonna win the race, well then nobody minds. He deserves it, that's fine. You even get guys from other crews wishing your driver luck. Which is funny. It's like being a gladiator and there's the lion, and you go wish the lion luck.

"DRIVERS, TO YOUR CARS"

Scott Dennison:

You develop a feeling for the driver, and realize that come racing time, there's a possibility that something could happen out there. You don't like to think about it, but nonetheless it's there. When you buckle him in for a race, you find there's a little more emotion involved than for practice, although the same thing could happen then as well. It's just one of those pat on the shoulder, "stand on the gas, and come back in one piece" kind of things.

Gordon Johncock:

There's one thing I don't like about the start of the Indy 500. I always like to know about three minutes before "Gentlemen start your engines," so I can put on my helmet and my gloves and my head sock, and get in the car. I just want to start it up, put it in gear, and leave, cause it's hot in the car. Once you get in there, you don't get any breeze. So you start sweating and it runs down in your eyes. Sometimes you have to flip up your shield, take your gloves, and wipe off the sweat, which is burning your eyes. Sometimes you sit there five to ten minutes waiting, and I think you get a little frustrated. Maybe even a little angry.

Howard Gilbert:

Everybody has a certain amount of respect for the driver and what he's doing. A lot of times it's a touch of the hand, a nod of the head. A lot of times nothing needs to be said. It's a feeling that goes with any team. When the guy's going out and putting his life on the line, you have a certain amount of respect that words don't begin to cover.

144

Bobby Rahal:

We're in this thing together. When I shake hands with my crew or they pat me, that's saying, "We're with you. Let's go get 'em!" I say it's a team thing. If we win today, it's we won, not I won.

Mario Andretti:

I think there is a drastic personality change when you climb into a race car. You don't become a madman, but you become aggressive enough so that you become extremely selfish. Even though you and I are good buddies, once we go out on the racetrack I'm not, just for the sake of getting an advantage, going to knock you off and try to hurt you. But you are not going to get an inch from me. Not any more than I think you should have. And I think out of that you acquire the respect and admiration for the other men as well.

AM 10:42

Michael Andretti:

It doesn't intimidate me, I just go out and do my own thing. You try not to let the other guys psych you out, but there are times when they try. Sometimes, if the situation's right, I'll try to psych the other guy out, depending on who he is. If it's somebody you've heard stories about, or had a problem with before, you better watch him carefully. But if it's somebody you can really trust, that's different. If it's a road race, you're trying to warm up the brakes, so when you get down the first lap they're there for you. Say you're coming into a corner, maybe you give the guy a little room up ahead, then fly into that corner and get a little friction on the tires.

AM 10:51

George Snider, Driver:

I think a guy gets a little nervous when he's thrown in the race car and they say, "Gentlemen, start your engines." I think everybody to a certain extent gets a butterfly in his stomach until the motor starts—because of the idea of hearing them say that. I can remember hearing it on the radio as a little boy. It got to me back then and still does a little bit.

Mario Andretti:

Things are already beginning to settle down inside of you, now that you're moving. You are checking things, everything is already happening, and it is much more relaxed. You are already in motion for the job. A lot of guys like to come over and give you the wave and stuff like that. I very seldom do it. The guy next to me is a robot, and that's the way he is treated. I don't care who it is. No wave, no blink of the eye, nothing. That is the way it goes. None of this friendly bullshit.

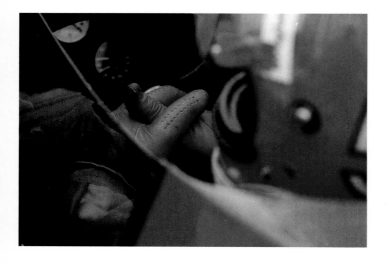

Bobby Rahal:

You're making sure the temperatures are coming up, and that the boost gauge is reading what you want it to read. Warm up the brakes...put your foot on the pedal. Scrub the tires a little bit. On an oval, the heat generates pretty quickly. You're just getting a feeling for the car. I consider it my friend when I get in. I say, "Okay, old boy, let's go!" It's all the little things you have to do before you go.

Bill Simpson:

On the pace lap I'm not doing anything except looking ahead and concentrating on what the start is going to be, how these guys line up, what is the lay of the land at this moment. It changes from second to second. By the time I'm over in the third corner, going around to get the green, my boost is up. I'm running 7,500 rpm and my brakes are smoking, because I'm running the brake and the gas at the same time, and I'm ready. When it goes green, I'm on my way.

Above: The starting field parades down Shoreline Drive and through "turn one" at Long Beach.

PARADE TO THE START

A. J. Foyt, Driver:

I am usually checking the clutch and the brakes, looking at the tires, and just waiting to come down for the start. I think that most people who talk about intimidating the other guy are pretty stupid. It's pretty dumb when they say they won't let nobody get by or move or nothing like that. He's trying to be a bully and just kind of lying to himself, because deep down in his heart he is probably a little yellow coward, to me. I have never had anybody try to do that to me. And if they acted real smart, like a bully with a race car, I would feel like driving it right through them. I wouldn't even put up with their crap, because they're just making conversation.

Rick Mears:

Some guys make these dive starts. It's stupid. I can't believe it. The engine's cold. The gear box is cold. The shocks are cold. Everything is cold. So I run the thing to about nine grand and shift it. I've had guys go past me clearing ten-five, just screaming the things. I back off and I shift slow, and they're revving gears and banging shifts, and I think, "Jesus Christ!" It's senseless. The first lap means nothing. Nobody remembers who leads the first lap. Well, I mean they remember it, but it's the last one that counts.

Below: Al Holbert at Portland International Raceway.

GOING GREEN

Wally Dallenbach:

By the first turn you're okay. It's been a long time since wrecks have happened there, but it's that sudden explosion of speed and power at the start/finish line. Thirty-three cars in eleven rows looking for power, gears, and boost. It's a dynamite time.

Mario Andretti:

People say the race is not won on the first lap. How true. I find I have to remind myself of that, because of my tendency to really stand on it. I mean, I want to lead. If I hang back, it's because I just can't go any further, not because I am willing to stay there. If I see a hole I don't wait for the other guy to go for it. I go for it, I guarantee you.

AM 11:00

Above: Looking over Bill Vukovich's shoulder at the start of the California 500 at Ontario Motor Speedway. *Below:* The rest of the field chases the leaders down the front straight at Indianapolis.

Gordon Johncock:

It's easier to anticipate a green flag somewhere like Milwaukee or Phoenix, because you have a real short straightaway. You're not too far out of the corner, and they got to drop it before you get underneath them. So the guys in the front row can see it, and there you kind of know. But when you get to Indianapolis, it's a little hard to anticipate. I think you have the biggest advantage starting on the pole, because you bring the cars down at the speed you want. One year at Indianapolis, Foyt was on the pole, I was second, and Bobby Unser was third. We were coming down for the green flag and I think maybe A. J. was trying to psych Bobby and me out just a bit. He got on the throttle to make an effort like he was going to go, so we got on the throttle like we were going to go. But A. J. backed out of it thinking, "If I get back out of it, they're going to do the same thing. Then I'm gonna jump back in while they're down." It didn't work that way. A. J. went out of sight on the left side of me when he did that. My eye was on Bobby, and Bobby didn't back off, so I didn't either. I just kept my foot on it, and I was the first one into the corner.

Bobby Unser:

When the car is handling good, I have a good chance of winning any race. Some of these other guys with fast cars aren't easy to beat, and I don't know if I could beat them every time. But I'm gonna be on the leader like a chicken on a june bug.

Below: A. J. Foyt at Pocono International Raceway. *Bottom:* Mario Andretti leads at Michigan International Speedway.

Above: Tom Sneva leads a pack of competitors through the first turn on the first lap of the 1981 Indy 500, as seen from a camera mounted on the rear of Vern Schuppan's car.

Dan Gurney:

There's a weapon that can be used in racing. It's a psychological thing, and it always remains a bit of an unknown. If the other drivers think you're ready to drive them off the track, should the opportunity present itself, they may back out of it before you ever have to get to that point. But if they're convinced the other way, they may stick their noses in there first.

Overleaf: A panorama from 100 feet above the first turn at the start of the Indianapolis 500.

BUGMEN AND THE TOOLS OF THEIR TRADE

Rouem Haffenden, Crew Chief:

The first lap is probably the worst. If anything's going to go wrong—if it's been forgotten or not done properly— the first lap's going to tell you. When they drop the flag and the guy comes around the first lap and it goes right, that's probably the biggest relief.

The refuelers work with harmful methanol fumes and the constant threat of fire, so they cover their bodies and faces with protective clothing and helmets with fire-retardant "skirts" attached.

Scott Dennison:

You've laid out the pit so that the car stops in a particular spot. We paint an arrow on the ground, so you know when you stand at that arrow and the car stops, the filler coupling on it is going to be in the right place. You also have to figure out if he over-shoots the pit, how far can he overshoot, and can you still reach him with the fuel hose? Or if he stops short, how far short can he be? He could overshoot the stopping point, and the jack man will have the car up in the air, and you can't reach him with the fuel. Then you've got to drop the car back down and roll it backwards. So you have to try to anticipate things like that.

Derek Mower, Crew Chief:

You wonder what's gonna go wrong, what will happen this time? You're just hoping you get everything handled. Cause that's your baby, and mechanics make the breaks or break it in the pits. You just make yourself say, "I'd better take it easy." Because if you rush your pit, if you try and be too smart about it or try to be too quick, the chances of making a mistake are far greater. We can change both tires in twelve seconds. You know it's going to take longer than that to put in fuel, so you don't have to do it that quick. The longer the race goes, the less fuel you have in your tanks and it will take even longer to refuel. So the first two stops are the most critical as far as tire changes. But then as the race goes on, you can afford to be careful.

Leo Mehl:

On race day they'll have a number of tires with various staggers in the pits, probably four sets of spares, plus what they start with—the same set they qualify on. If they develop a pushing condition, or a loose rear-end condition during the race, they can actually adjust the chassis by putting on a different diameter tire. Many guys have won races with their ability to think under the heat of competition, and figure out what's wrong and what the solution might be in regards to changing tires.

George Heuning:

The time it's the worst is when everybody's about due for a pit stop. You're getting the mileage and everybody knows within two or three laps when everybody's gotta stop. On a big track, it works out to about twenty-six laps under a green. So on the twentieth lap, if the yellow comes out almost every car on the racetrack dives into the pits. That's when I really try to keep my eyes open, cause there are race cars going just everywhere. The driver looks for our uniforms and our signboards, because there are so many uniforms along pit row. Everybody's wearing colors. You can't really tell where your crew is at. He's coming in pretty hot, and as fast as he can, so you don't lose any more time than you have to. You'd think an airplane was coming in for a landing. Usually I make some motions.

Top to bottom: The front- and rear-tire men handle 20-pound impact wrenches; a single nut fixes each wheel to the axle. Yards of air hose trail behind the gun.

The main fuel nozzle assembly is attached to a ten-foot length of three-inch-diameter rubber hosing that leads to the fuel storage tank. The nozzle plugs into the car's filler coupling. When it is pulled free, an "auto close" valve, spring-loaded dry-break apparatus with an inner-sleeve assembly snaps shut to prevent spillage. With five gallons already in the hose, the assembly hefted by the "fueler" weighs about fifty pounds.

The two-inch-diameter vent nozzle assembly also incorporates a check valve, as well as a clear "window" through which the "ventman" can see the bubbling fuel that signals his pull-out. The ventman also wields the air hose, with an automatic-coupling device at the end, for the jacks.

When the air hose is plugged in, air compressed under 250 psi flows to four pneumatic jack assemblies. The 1¾-inch aluminum shafts lift the car just high enough to enable tire changes.

Above: Riding with A. J. Foyt at Indianapolis.

Phil Casey:

You talk back and forth over the radio, and if he's having any problems he'll tell you. If it gets loose, you plan on changing the stagger in the rear a little bit with a different size tire. If the thing starts pushing on him, you can't do it with a stagger. Then you'll try to stick some more wing in it or something. The driver can adjust the roll bars and dial some of it out himself.

George Snider:

A pit stop can be hard on you, because you're wanting to go and you can't. They aren't done yet. You got your motor and yourself running pretty hard, and to me it's really not a rest. You're wanting to go harder and get out of there as quick as you can. Your brain is still running at full speed.

Rick Mears:

When I get in a tangle with somebody, and he's holding me up, I'm getting mad. As soon as I can get by, and his car goes out of my peripheral vision, he goes out of my mind. He's not there anymore. I'm already thinking about what I'm doing up here. You're constantly moving ahead. I'm no sooner past one car, then I'm thinking about who's the next guy up there. What am I going to have to do? How am I going to approach him? How's he running? Where's he working? Where am I working? Where's my best way to get him? Priorities.

Bobby Rahal:

You trust your instincts, and they'll tell you that there are some people you can bank on, and others you're not sure what they're gonna do. You can see who it is, and what car it is, so you make the appropriate judgment at that point in time.

Bill Simpson:

Do you know how big a set of balls a guy has to have to stand up there at the right front and signal where you've got to stop? He's watching this projectile hurtling at him at a hundred miles an hour or better, knowing that in fifty or sixty yards that car will stop dead right where his hand is. He has that much faith in you.

Rick Mears:

As I get close, I start getting on the binders, and I throw the thing out of gear. When you come in like that and you're shifting, you got to use your left foot on the clutch and the right foot on the brake. Then I want to make sure I don't kill it.

COMING IN

Above: Derek Daly pulls in for his first scheduled pit stop.

George Heuning:

It takes a second or two for that nut to move after you get the wrench on and start hammering, so you can be on that thing going the wrong way before it dawns on you that it isn't moving. And meanwhile that's two seconds lost. So when I'm changing the tire, I'm constantly looking down at the air gun, pulling that trigger, and I'm making sure it's going the right way.

Rick Mears:

It's a helpless feeling. There's nothing you can do. When that car gets away, the guy's along for the ride. Nine times out of ten he's got his head down and his eyes shut.

"YELLOW, YELLOW, YELLOW"

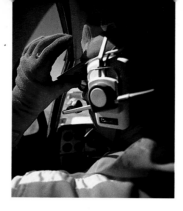

Steve Edwards, Safety Director:

That adrenaline flow is important. It keeps you on your toes and makes you what you are. At the same time you can't come unglued at what you may see. When a car hits the wall at two hundred miles an hour, no matter how well-built it is, you can't anticipate how bad it's going to be.

Above: Steve Edwards, the Championship Auto Racing Teams' safety director, and Dr. Steve Olvey, CART medical director, speed to the crash site.

Gordon Johncock:

One little mistake can cost you your life. You're going two hundred miles an hour. One wrong move and you're either into the wall or somebody hits you. You don't usually get a second chance.

Steve Edwards:

Fire. Medical. Extrication. Cleanup. All those things have to begin to happen at the same time, with priority given to the fire and medical aspects. Because the driver is your number one consideration. You're beginning to think in advance about coordinating people and the steps you're going to have to go through. All that flashes through your mind at one time.

Michael Andretti:

I just try to block it out, and hope it's not my turn. I still feel when it's your time, it's your time.

Steve Edwards:

Under full blaze conditions, that suit can offer protection for thirty seconds. That doesn't mean the driver isn't going to be in any kind of hazard. He can't take a full-force blast of fire for thirty seconds. What they are really saying is, it will be about that long before the fire burns through the suit. You don't want to work with those kinds of numbers. In my own mind, after five seconds you're going to start having harm done, even if it's nothing more than his visor beginning to melt.

Mike Mosley:

The first time I got hurt, I came in and told them, "It scared me." Every time I came out of the same corner, I could just see it happen again. And the worst are the ones that you remember. You can't get scared if you don't realize what happened.

Steve Edwards:

When you first come to the car and you see its condition, you begin to read how it hit the wall. You often get front bulkheads or pedals folded around the feet, so maybe you have a potential broken foot, ankle, or leg. Maybe the tub has compressed around the legs, so you have a situation where you're going to have to free them. Depending on what kind of shot he took from the side, you're always looking for a head injury. You assess him for vital signs before you do anything else. He's not going to die of a broken ankle, but if he's not breathing or his heart's stopped, he's going to die from that. So you're going to treat the priorities the same, irrespective of what the crash is like. Whether he's upside down, or just spun and tore a wheel off the car, or took a full-force shot into the wall.

To free the legs of a driver trapped in twisted wreckage. the Hurst Tool is used. Called the "Jaws of Life" by those who depend on it. the tool can either compress metal or pry it apart with titanium fingers. A portable generator pumps hydraulic fluid to power the tool with 12.000 pounds of pressure.

Al Unser, Sr.:

I have no death wish. There is nothing that frightens me more than to crash. I don't want to get hurt in any manner, shape, or form. Every time I crash, when I get out of that car and I'm able to get out of it, I say, "Thank God I'm here." And I do thank Him, because I believe in God, and the good Lord rides with us all.

Scott Dennison:

Yellow flags become so critical in races. If you have to pit under the green you really lose a lot of time. If you pit under the yellow all you lose is the distance between the front and the back of the pack when everybody groups up, and you haven't lost much. There's a lot of strategy involved. Say you're scheduled to come in for fuel at the sixtieth lap, you hope that at the fifty-fifth or fifty-eighth lap you'll get a yellow, so it works into your schedule. Otherwise you could get screwed. You may come in on the sixtieth lap, go back out and on the sixty-second lap get a yellow. Then you've lost a lap. You really don't have any control over that. You just try to plan to your best advantage. There's a lot of luck in this business.

Mario Andretti:

When I drop out early I could just scream for a half hour straight, to get it off my chest. You could just cry a thousand times. I've told my wife that I feel my heart is breaking and the cracks are as big as some of the ones in the pavement. It's a tremendous disappointment.

Richard Fried:

You put out all your effort—work your ass off—and you're leading the race after 140 laps, and the engine breaks. It just breaks. Or some idiot blows his motor in front of you, and you spin out and wreck your car on his oil. It's got nothing to do with you or your driver or your car. It's just that you happened to be in the wrong place at the wrong time.

Rick Mears:

I keep it running with my right foot. My left foot's on the brake, as they jack it up. That way the wheels don't spin when they're trying to take them off. When I see they're about halfway through changing the tires and stuff, I'll slide my right foot half off the throttle and onto the brake. I keep it going with my heel and put brake pressure on with my toe. My left foot slides over to the clutch, because I'm trying to get it in gear before they're through. This is all happening within eight seconds. You want it to be in gear and ready to go when it hits the ground. You can hear when they're through with the wheels, the air guns quit working. Then you know you don't have to worry about the tires spinning anymore. Slide your foot off the brake and fully onto the throttle, so you have good foot control to keep it running. So it won't die on you. Be ready as soon as that thing hits the ground. You're on your way.

Wally Dallenbach:

The only time I ever see any intimidation is on restarts. And it usually comes from a guy in the lead who wound up in the back of the pack after a fuel stop. So he threatens. He lets the guy in front of him know that he's about to be blown off when that flag comes down. He usually comes up on the side he's going to do it on.

Rick Mears:

Something pissed me off once halfway through a race, and I ran harder when I was mad. It may help if I go out there and get thoroughly pissed off before I get in the car. I may go like a bomb. But then I may stick her in the fence, too. So I always go the other way. I'm calming myself down all the time. Relax. Take it easy. I've a long way to go. A lot of time. The more keyed up you get, the more psyched you get, and the more pumped up you get, the more apt you are to make a mistake. The first half of the race I'm usually cussing the car, and the second half I'm really being nice to it. The first half you're trying to make it go quicker. Later on, you're saying, "Come on baby, please get to the end."

George Snider:

I've never been really hard on strategy. You just run as fast as you can go the whole race. It seems when you make up a plan to hold a conservative pace for fifty laps because you figure ten guys are going to drop out, it doesn't work. All ten of them stay in, and you're running last.

Bobby Rahal:

It's like in running when they talk about the wall. In a marathon it's ten or fifteen miles, and once you've broken through it's okay. In a five hundred-mile race you hit it at two hundred miles. You see the lap board and think, "God...125 more laps to go!" You're always embroiled in a battle, or you're trying to catch somebody or leave somebody, and pretty soon it starts. But if you're mentally tough, then it's not a problem. Certainly you're going to feel the heat, and you're going to be tired, but you can stave off those feelings until the end of the race. Mentally you can say, "I'm not tired, I'm not hot." If you're concentrating as you should be, you're all right.

PM 12:16

Mario Andretti:

A pit stop? A royal pain in the ass. It's the only way I can truthfully describe it. I find you're exposed to so many mistakes. No matter how good your crew is, mistakes are made, and you wind up paying for it dearly. I would rather be out there, calculating the rhythm of the race and getting into a pattern. Coming in and starting all over again really irritates me.

Johnny Rutherford, Driver:

It's a precision drill, very much like airplanes flying formation. Probably the hardest thing is finding your pit. Really, you don't find it until the last minute, but you've got to keep your speed up and still make the transition. You're slowing, just like a clock winding down, as you roll in and stop. The car comes up while they're changing tires and you've got to keep your foot on the brake, the engine running, the car ready to go in gear. I keep an eye on the fuel man watching the vent line, because when he makes his move, you're very close. I start getting the gearshift manipulated to the right spot before the car is down off the jacks. Then I go with the other foot to the clutch and start sneaking it into gear, so when they wave me go, I can drop the hammer and be gone.

Richard Fried:

The first time I ever did a pit stop it was over in an instant. Now I have enough time to look at all the tires and at what everybody's doing. Because I handle the vent hose, I can look down at the gauges in the cockpit, and at the fueler, while I wait for the fuel to come up. "Boy, this is taking a long time!" You pull out, and it's a fifteen-second stop!

Above and top right: Motion studies accomplished with a Widelux panoramic camera.

Michael Andretti:

If fumes start coming in these cars, it's terrible. You start losing any sense of where you are, your eyes start tearing, your lungs burn, and that screws you up a lot. That's the worst part. Usually once it starts coming down off the jacks, I'm putting it in gear, trying to get the revs up. If you break the tires loose evenly, you'll be all right getting out.

Bill Simpson:

I don't think there is anything more satisfying than an organization that operates just like a spider. It's five guys who are individual, like legs, but it's one body. They're all operating to do the same thing. It's amazing that it can all be done as quickly as it is.

The Victory Circle platform at Indianapolis is constructed as the race draws toward conclusion. The fastening down of the checkered carpet, the last stage in the platform's construction, accompanies pit-stop activity just outside the barriers.

Michael Andretti:

Funny thing is, if you're in the lead and running well, you start hearing things by the end of the race. It's very loud in the car with a whining, vibrating sound, and while you know you've been hearing these sounds the whole race, all of a sudden you think, "Boy, that sounds a little different."

Rick Mears:

As it starts getting close to the end, we're going to start getting set up here. We're going to start getting into the position we want. So I start to run a little harder, and I'm running right by the leader. Okay, we're going to have to stay close here and start making some moves pretty quick. I start talking to myself. I start getting a little "racier." I start pumping myself a little bit, but then he "breaks." So I go back to running my pace, my speed. But if he hadn't broken, then by the last five to ten laps I'd have gotten racy. It would have been a dandy if he didn't break and we'd have a hell of a battle. But, see, there's no sense waging a battle like that until you have to, cause that's when you get into trouble. I see guys just thrash and bang and go on, ten laps into the race. Jesus, why do that? Save that for last, when

Tom Sneva:

You're just hoping that things are going to stay together. You know if they do, then you are going to win. You're concerned about things falling off, or the engine breaking, or having a tire go, or something. But fortunately when it's your day, it seems like it's your day all the way around. The car is handling right from the start.

Howard Gilbert:

It's one of the greatest feelings in the world. It's something you can't describe to anybody. All the anticipations and fears just leave you all at once, replaced by another thing—happiness, joy. There's only one who wins. It's too bad that there are people who have raced at Indianapolis half a lifetime and have never experienced that feeling of great achievement.

Team McLaren wins the 1974 Pocono 500 as Johnny Rutherford crosses the finish line first.

Scott Dennison:

It's the most fantastic feeling in the world. You've put so much time in it and are so involved, that if your car wins, the initial response is just total berzerko.

Above: The Newman/Haas team reacts to Mario Andretti's win over Tom Sneva in the 1984 Michigan 500, the closest finish in Indy car history.

Below: Johnny Rutherford notches his third Indy 500 win in the Chaparral in 1980.

Richard Fried:

That's it! Ha, ha, sons of bitches—we blew your doors off! I enjoy being top dog. I mean that's what we're out there for, to win.

Above: In 1977 A. J. Foyt became the Indy 500's only four-time winner.

Jim Hall:

Winning is a real, real rush, you know? It's a tremendous high and a feeling of accomplishment, because there's an awful lot of work that goes into it. It starts from the very beginning with the idea of building a car, and then goes on to putting the whole thing together, and getting it working. Your whole effort for a considerable number of months has been pretty much undivided toward that end.

Mario Andretti:

Like it or hate it, Indianapolis is there, and winning it is one of the most satisfying moments of a man's career. You want that race so bad, you can taste it. And when you finally achieve it, no matter how, you feel a big glow is offered you, and you figure, "Well, that baby is in the bag." The next one, whatever comes from then on, is a bonus. Man, everything is all right after that. The world can break in two pieces, and it's still a lovely day.

PM 2:31

George Heuning:

All we could do was gather up a lot of sheet metal. That was all that was left of the car. We tried to get it into the garage and out of sight, but the photographers were acting just like a pack of hungry wolves. I came walking back from the crash with my driver's helmet under my arm, and it was like I was a piece of raw meat. At that point, if I had a gun, I would have started shooting.

Bobby Rahal:

The highs in this sport are so high and the lows are so devastating. Luckily, the highs are higher. You may have many disappointments, but when you win, those disappointments are no longer in view. You've forgotten about them.

Mario Andretti:

Winning is the only thing you can keep score on, and I am one who just doesn't accept anything less for myself. I want to climb that tree and get to the very top of it. Some of those limbs up there I know can be awfully flimsy. But you're never going to reach the top unless you step on a few, and hope to hell they don't break. You've got to take those chances, otherwise you'll remain in the middle of the tree, and you can't see worth a damn from there.